and

LEADERSHIP

a manual for walkers

The Ramblers

Published by the Ramblers' Association, 1/5 Wandsworth Road, London, SW8 2XX
Phone: 071-582 6878

Text by Colin Saunders

Cartoons by Martin Shovel
Design by Julian Tippett and AdCity, 081-546 1363

Printed and bound in Great Britain by Sharpe Print, Buntingford, Hertfordshire

ISBN 0-900613-76-9

ACKNOWLEDGEMENTS

This manual has been compiled under the auspices of the Ramblers' Association Panel of Advisers on Navigation and Leadership: Jo Bird, Nick Chetwood, Geoff Eastwood, Geoff Elliott, Brian Nelson, Chris Sweetman, Julian Tippett.

Further help or advice has been provided particularly by: The Ackers, Birmingham; British Orienteering Federation; Central Council of Physical Recreation; Metropolitan Police; Ordnance Survey; Ramblers' Association areas – Kent, Leicestershire, London and West Riding; St.John Ambulance; Iain Peter, United Kingdom Mountain Training Board; also – Robert Pettigrew.

Members and staff of the Ramblers' Association contributed.

Photographs are reproduced by the permission of the following: page 9 – English Wanderer Walking Holidays; page 68 – Bucks Free Press; page 75 – Geoff King; page 82 – Basingstoke Gazette Newspapers; page 95 – The News, Portsmouth.

The 'Bull Chart' on page 78 is reproduced by permission of *The Countryman* in which it first appeared.

Figures 5, 7, 9, 11, 12 and 17 are reproduced by permission of The Duke of Edinburgh's Award and Wally Keay; they first appeared in Mr Keay's book 'Land Navigation', published by the Award.

Figures 2, 3, 4, 6, 13, 15 and 16 by Julian Tippett.

The syllabi in boxes 20 and 21 by Julian Tippett and Brian Nelson, respectively.

ENVIRONMENTALLY FRIENDLY PAPER

The bleaches used for making the paper in this book are totally chlorine-free.

CONTENTS

List of Figures and Boxes

The Ramblers' Association

Aims and Activities

The Ramblers' Association exists to protect the interests of everyone who enjoys walking in the countryside. Since 1935, The Ramblers' Association has promoted rambling, protected footpaths, sought public access to open country, encouraged respect for the countryside and defended its natural beauty.

Today the Association has over 96,000 members, more than 360 local RA groups and over 800 affiliated clubs and societies.

Local Ramblers' groups organise programmes of walks which you are welcome to join. They also keep an eye on what is happening in their local countryside, monitoring the state of footpaths and campaigning for more access to open country.

Members receive copies of the quarterly colour magazine Rambling Today and the annual Rambler's Yearbook and Accommodation Guide. They also get regular campaign broadsheets and local newsletters and can make use of our Landranger and Outdoor Leisure OS map library.

The Association depends almost entirely for its income on the subscriptions, donations and legacies of its members and supporters.

Further details of membership can be obtained from the address on the rear cover of this manual.

Foreword

Walking in the countryside continues to be Britain's most popular recreation, and its popularity continues to grow.

Much of the recent growth of the Ramblers' Association has been derived from the increase in the size and number of its local groups. Those groups – nearly 400 of them – offer an astonishingly varied and imaginative programme of walks to their members. The groups are fortunate in having many volunteers to call upon to plan and lead walks.

But some groups need more leaders. Volunteers can often be found, but many need training and advice on navigation and leadership before feeling fully confident about taking a party of walkers into the countryside. We hope that this manual will provide that advice, and offer material for simple, effective training programmes.

This manual is therefore intended primarily for Areas and Groups of the Ramblers' Association. It has been produced in response to requests from them. However, we hope that the manual will also be of use to independent walking groups and clubs outside the Ramblers' Association. There are probably thousands of them throughout Britain, and their moral and material support for the RA's work of protecting rights of way, access and the countryside is greatly appreciated.

We hope that the manual will be useful to individual walkers as well. It has been written in a way that facilitates self-tuition in the subjects that it covers.

The pages that follow are the distillation of the considerable body of knowledge and experience in these matters which members of the Ramblers' Association in our Areas and Groups have built up over the years. But the preparation of this manual has been undertaken in a spirit of humility and willingness to learn. We do not pretend to offer the last word on navigation and leadership. Nor does this manual provide the basis for any formal qualification in navigation and walks leadership. It is stressed throughout that the guidance offered here is relevant mainly to 'moderate' walking conditions. Further advice must be sought for leading walks in winter conditions in the hills – especially in remote areas, such as the highlands of Scotland.

The importance and value of being able to find your way competently over all types of terrain, using map and compass, cannot be overestimated. Walking is the best way of discovering and exploring the countryside (and, for that matter, urban areas as well), and skill in navigation techniques is your passport to that adventure.

Alan Mattingly
Director, The Ramblers' Association
October 1993

Introduction

Purpose of the manual

1 Since its foundation in 1935, the **Ramblers' Association** (the RA) has grown to become the voice of Britain's most popular outdoor recreation, enjoyed by a quarter of the population, and is recognised as the acknowledged authority on footpath and access matters. With an individual membership fast approaching 100,000 and with an integrated regional structure, it is in an excellent position to communicate the vast experience of its members to those who wish to organise and lead walks, or to improve their navigation and leadership techniques, or teach others to do so.

2 This manual is primarily intended for **RA members** who wish to improve their navigation, or to become leaders, or both. But it will also be of use to anyone, RA member or not, who wishes to increase his or her enjoyment of walking, or to share it with others. It will help those who have only recently taken up walking, and just want to learn how to

On the coastal path above Morfa Harlech, the mountains of Snowdonia in the distance

read a map, then take family, friends or colleagues on a walk near home, whether in the countryside, or along an urban "green chain".

3 Of course, we hope that **non-members** will discover how much the RA works on their behalf, and decide to join.

A phone call suffices to ask the RA national office to post an application form (071-582 6878).

4 Members of an **RA group or affiliated rambling club** are probably only too familiar with that plaintive cry from the committee, "More leaders please!" This manual, by offering instruction, advice and encouragement, provides an opportunity for readers to respond. And it can be used by those same committees as the basis for informal learning sessions and as encouragement for their members. The section on organising and running a course shows them how to set about it.

5 The manual can be used in the same way by other organisations, such as **youth or community groups**, to extend their range of activities.

6 **Experienced leaders** may also find in this manual some suggestions and advice for situations which they have not as yet encountered, or in which they have felt uncomfortable.

7 We stress that this manual provides instruction on how to navigate and lead in what we call **"moderate conditions"** (see below). It does not cover "wild conditions", such as on mountains or isolated moorland, or in severe winter conditions. For this, a considerable amount of experience is necessary, possibly backed up by undertaking one of the award schemes or courses listed in appendix 2.

8 The manual furthers the **constitutional aim** of the RA to promote walking to all sections of the community. We hope that readers will be encouraged to plan their own walks. Then, through gradually gained experience, they may feel confident enough to take on the responsibility of leading, thus helping others to enjoy this absorbing and healthy activity.

9 **Leading** is by no means all responsibility and work. It can be great fun, and at the end of the day gives the satisfaction of knowing that other walkers have also had a good day out. As well as giving advice on how to lead, the manual shows how to get the most enjoyment and satisfaction out of leading.

Moderate conditions

10 The aim of this manual is to provide readers with the basic skills needed to navigate and lead in **moderate conditions**. It does *not* include skills for "wild" conditions, i.e:

- areas where a high degree of navigational skill is required, such as mountainous or hazardous terrain, or remote areas.
- routes involving sustained "scrambling" (where hands as well as feet must be used for ascent or descent).
- walking in severe winter conditions.
- walks involving backpacking and overnight camping.

Awards

11 By design, no award or certificate will be presented to those who learn solely from this manual. Nor is one necessary to plan a walk in moderate conditions, or to be accepted as a leader by your group or club. **Proficiency in navigation and leadership** comes, not only by learning from a book, but also through plenty of practical experience "on the ground".

Even then, the unexpected can happen, and experienced walkers have no reason for being careless or complacent, especially when leading other people in the countryside.

12 Those who need or wish to gain an award or certificate can do so by participating in one of the **award schemes or courses** listed in appendix 2.

How to use this manual

13 A section covers each of Navigation and Leadership and, for those whose ambition extends to teaching others, a third section on Training shows how to organise and run a course.

14 The **Navigation** section shows how to use a map and compass, and how to plan a route in the moderate conditions described above. It will also encourage you to incorporate lesser-used footpaths, helping to keep them open, and as a change from the more regularly used ones. Experienced walkers will not need all the material, but are recommended to skim it carefully, as they may still learn something useful.

15 The **Leadership** section shows how to prepare for your walk, what should or could happen on the day itself, how to manage the party, what to do if there is a problem, and how leading a walk for the public differs from leading for your group or club. This section will help you to exercise the "Duty of Care" placed upon anyone taking a party into the countryside.

16 The section on **Training** covers the whole procedure of **organising and running a course**, from making contact with your local authority or RA group, and getting hold of equipment, to teaching in the classroom and practical outdoor work, using the modules in this manual.

17 Sections are divided into **modules**, relating to various aspects of the subject. For ease of reference, each paragraph within a module is numbered, and its main theme highlighted in bold print. Cross references to paragraphs give module number and paragraph number, e.g. "see paragraph 3.14" refers to module 3, paragraph 14.

18 If you are planning to lead a walk in **Scotland**, you should obtain a leaflet entitled "Leading RA Walking Parties in Scotland". For a copy, please send a large stamped addressed envelope to the RA Scottish Office (see appendix 5).

19 A number of **practical exercises** suitable for individual or class use, are included at the end of modules 1 and 2. Others, suitable for class use only, are shown at the end of the module on organising and running a course.

Box 1 **Leading in Europe**

Whilst this manual has been written with particular regard to walking in the United Kingdom, the general principles of navigation and leadership as described apply virtually anywhere in Europe under moderate conditions (see Introduction, paragraph 10).

However, there are important national differences in rights and traditions of access and use of footpaths, which may affect map reading and route planning. It may be worth contacting the appropriate regional or national tourist office (see appendix 5), as many produce literature containing advice about walking in those areas.

Please bear in mind that the RA's public liability insurance (see paragraph 4.4) applies only to walks taking place in the United Kingdom (i.e. England, Wales, Scotland, the Channel Islands, the Isle of Man and Northern Ireland). If you are leading elsewhere (including the Republic of Ireland), you are advised to take out suitable insurance cover for public liability.

SECTION A: NAVIGATION

Module 1: Map reading

1 **Navigation** can be described as the art of finding one's way around unknown territory. To do this you can either undertake the lengthy and tiresome process of trial and error, you can follow a walking guide book, or you can use a map. Once you have mastered its intricacies, you will find map reading by far the easiest and most reliable way of navigating.

Maps

2 A **map** represents at a reduced scale a chosen part of the earth's surface. It can show any features or landmarks of the area, as desired by the map-maker, but the ones we are concerned with are the physical ones – those you can see – such as roads, buildings, bridges, woods and footpaths.

3 The **scale** of a map indicates the amount by which real distance has been reduced to fit on it. The commonest map scales used by walkers are:

1:25,000 – one centimetre on the map represents 25,000 centimetres or 250 metres on the ground; and 4 millimetres represents 100 metres.

1:50,000 – one centimetre on the map represents 50,000 centimetres or 500 metres on the ground; and 2 millimetres represents 100 metres.

Note: In this manual, we use **metric measurements –** centimetres, metres and kilometres. One metre = 1.09 yards; one kilometre = 0.62 miles.

For a quick, rough conversion:

From metres to yards – add 10 per cent.

Kilometres to miles – divide by eight then multiply by five.

1 mile = 1.6 kilometres – or – 3 miles = 5 kilometres.

100 metres = 300 feet – or – 300 metres = 1,000 feet.

4 Most maps in Britain are published by the **Ordnance Survey** (commonly abbreviated to OS), a government agency based in Southampton. Their maps are sold in bookshops and outdoor equipment shops throughout the country, and there is also a number of specialist map shops, including some that offer a mail order service (see appendix 4).

5 The OS offers a very wide range of maps for various purposes; each kind is known as a **series**. Three of them are of particular interest to walkers:

> **Landranger** series (1:50,000 magenta cover).
>
> **Pathfinder** series (1:25,000 green cover).
>
> **Outdoor Leisure** series (1:25,000 yellow cover).

The Landranger and Pathfinder series cover the whole of Britain. Outdoor Leisure maps are published only for the most popular walking areas, and usually replace the Pathfinders where they overlap.

6 The **1:25,000 scale** is strongly recommended for walk leaders, because it shows much more detail – especially helpful in places where the line of a path may not otherwise be clear. The disadvantage of Pathfinder maps is that they do not cover such a wide area as the Landranger, so you may need to buy and carry more maps to cover your intended route. The disadvantage of Outdoor Leisure maps is that they are very large, and can be difficult to handle in bad weather. In England and Wales, rights of way (see paragraph 2.7) on both Pathfinder and Outdoor Leisure maps are shown in green. Permissive paths (see paragraph 2.8) may be shown in some other colour.

Shops might sell maps at the 1:25,000 scale only for their immediate locality, so for those covering areas further afield you may need to place an order, or obtain them by mail order (see appendix 4).

7 The **1:50,000 scale** Landranger maps are suitable for individual ramblers in hill or moorland areas with little mapped detail, and to give a wider overview of your walking area. They also give a better impression of topography or relief. However, in places where a lot of

detail has to be shown, you are likely to find that at this scale it is not possible to see exactly where your intended path goes. In England and Wales, rights of way are shown in broken red lines.

8 Individual maps within each series are known as **sheets**. For ease of reference, all map series have their own index system of sheet numbers. Those for both Pathfinders (sheet nos. 1-1372) and Landrangers (1-204) start at the north end of the British Isles (Shetland Isles) and work their way down to Cornwall. The Outdoor Leisure sheets are numbered in the order in which they were first published.

* Older Pathfinder sheets might be referenced by only an index number consisting of two letters followed by four figures, e.g. TQ 26/36. This old number is also shown in brackets after the new number, as well as on the index map (see paragraph 9 ii below).

9 To find out which **sheet number(s)** you need for your walk:

i Consult a road map or atlas to get a general picture of the area you wish to visit. Note particularly any towns or cities nearby.

ii Look at the index map for the appropriate series. All Landranger and Outdoor Leisure sheets include a complete index map on their back covers. Pathfinders, because there are so many more of them, only show the numbers of the sheet concerned and its neighbours; however, a separate index map for these is published free by the Ordnance Survey (telephone 0703-792763/4), and a copy is usually available for inspection at shops that sell maps.

iii From the index map, you can get a rough idea of which sheet(s) are required. Then you must look at the map itself to check that it covers exactly your walking area. When obtaining maps by post, you can use a Landranger map to check the precise coverage of a Pathfinder map – almost all of these cover pairs of adjacent 10 km grid squares.

10 Ordnance Survey maps are updated fairly regularly, and you should try to ensure that you have a **recent edition** – good bookshops usually sell the latest.

On Ordnance Survey maps you can check this in two ways:

i The year of publication is shown at the bottom left-hand corner of the map when folded out.

ii Towards the foot of the "key" (see paragraph 12 below), it says in what way the map has been revised and in which year.

The Ordnance Survey call their current maps the "Second Series", which are based fully on a metric scale. The "First Series" are recognisable by the words First Series on the cover and oddly numbered contour heights (converted into metres directly from 25 and 50 foot contour intervals). First Series maps should not be used as they are very much out of date. A few one-inch-to-one-mile maps are still published covering some national parks (in the Touring Map series), but they are not recommended for walking.

11 For some popular walking areas, maps are published by **independent publishers** and may be of a different scale, such as those published by Harveys at 1:40,000, which, incidentally, use waterproof paper. However, in this manual it is assumed that you will be using an Ordnance Survey map (at a scale of either 1:25,000 or 1:50,000) and where appropriate the text should be taken as referring to these.

12 The way in which physical features on a map are represented is shown in its **key**, usually found to one side of the map (on Landrangers and Pathfinders) or underneath it (Outdoor Leisure). The symbols you should pay particular attention to are those representing:

i Roads and paths; also public rights of way (except in Scotland).

ii Features – especially buildings, such as churches, and other features, such as electricity transmission (power) lines and railway lines.

iii Vegetation, especially woodland.

iv Heights ("contours" – see paragraphs 15 to 21 below).

v Water features.

These are the ones that will help you best to find your way. On Pathfinder and Outdoor Leisure maps, another useful symbol for walkers, though not shown in the key, is the fine black line representing field boundaries – usually a hedge, wall or fence. Remember, though, there is a chance of fences or hedges being removed since publication of the map.

13 Most maps are sold **folded,** and before going out you will re-fold them to show the required piece of territory. They can also be bought flat, making them easier to fold to your requirements. Most bookshops do not stock these, so they usually have to be ordered.

14 Unless your map is laminated, or made of waterproof paper, you should have some form of **map protection**. This is essential in wet weather, and keeps the map free of mud splashes. It could be home-made from a clear polythene bag, big enough to take your map when folded.

There are also purpose made **map-cases**, which can be bought at most outdoor equipment and specialist map shops. They range from simple clear plastic wallets to more substantial ones with pockets for compass, notebook, pencils etc. They are usually fastened with Velcro, and have a neckband.

Contours

15 A **contour** is a line connecting points of equal altitude, or height above sea level. Contours and their associated spot heights are the means used by the map-maker to portray the shape of the land, its height, the form taken by hills and valleys, steepness of slopes, and so on. On all Pathfinder and Outdoor Leisure maps, the interval between contours is usually 5 metres, but on sheets covering mountainous areas it is 10 metres, because the lines would otherwise be too close together. On Landrangers the interval is always 10 metres.

16 At random points along many of the contour lines, a number is shown to indicate its height, always printed so that the top of the number points uphill. However in some areas where a lot of detail has to be included, these numbers are not

frequent and you may have to follow the line along for some distance until you find one, or count up or down from another line which does show a number. Further help is provided by the fact that every fifth contour line is printed more thickly than the others.

17 As well as indicating the height above sea level, contours can:

i Enable you to pinpoint your position.

ii Tell you whether your route goes uphill, downhill or on the level at any given point.

Figure 2

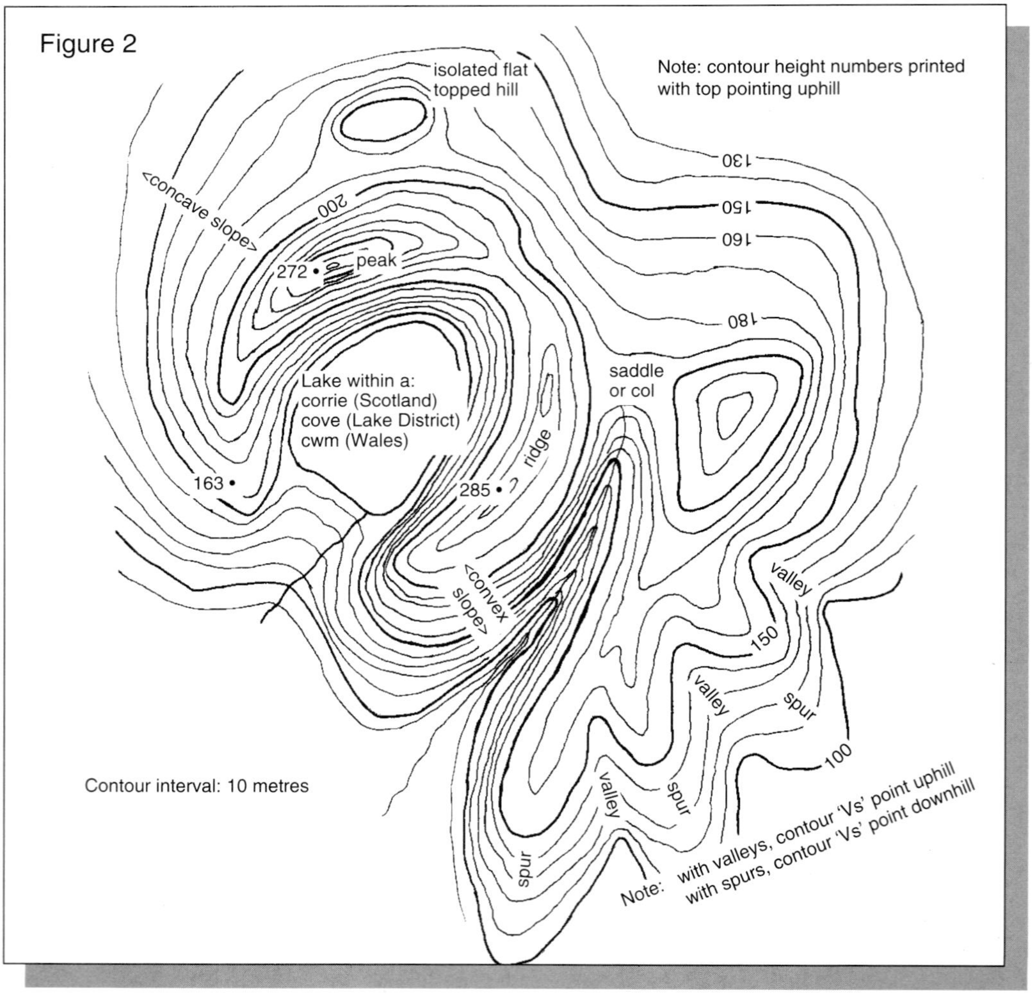

iii Show how much ascent and descent your route involves – this may affect the time you need to allow for your walk. To do this, you count the number of contours crossed, and note whether the route ascends or descends.

iv Show steepness – the closer together the contours are, the steeper the ascent or descent will be.

v Help you decide where to go when planning your route, by avoiding steep slopes or including hills with views, as required.

vi Enable you to identify distant land forms (see paragraph 19 below).

18 Contours show the **shape of the land** – see figure 2.

19 Contours enable you to identify **distant land forms**. For example, from a hilltop you can pick out neighbouring hills and valleys by comparing what you can see with the contours on the map. This can help you decide in which direction to continue.

20 **Spot heights**, shown as a number beside a dot, appear at strategic points, often along roads where they level out at the top or foot of a hill. These can be a useful guide where contour height numbers are infrequent.

21 **Trig point** is the commonly used abbreviation for a triangulation pillar – a place, usually on a hilltop, from where OS surveyors used to measure height and distance (nowadays they use satellite technology). They are marked on maps with their height in metres, and can usually be identified on the ground as distinctive concrete pillars a little over one metre high. Thus trig points can be a useful aid to walkers in pinpointing their position on the map.

However, the now redundant trig points, owned by the Ordnance Survey, have been offered for adoption by people or organisations who are prepared to maintain them. It is possible that some of those which are not adopted will in due course be removed, or fall into disrepair thus reducing their visibility from a distance.

Grid references

22 All Ordnance Survey maps are criss-crossed by vertical and horizontal **grid lines**. If they could be drawn on the ground, they would be exactly one kilometre apart. On the map, grid lines are 4 centimetres apart on the 1:25,000 scale; 2 centimetres apart on the 1:50,000 scale. On Pathfinder maps they are black; on Landranger and Outdoor Leisure maps, blue.

23 Grid lines are so-called after the **national grid** whose origin lies at a point in the Atlantic Ocean to the south-west of the Scilly Isles. The vertical ones are called *eastings* (because they progress eastwards from the point of origin), and the horizontal ones *northings* (which progress northwards).

24 A **grid reference** (often abbreviated to "GR") is a useful means of identifying a particular spot on the map – or more accurately an area 100 metres square. They can help when discussing a route with someone over the telephone or in a letter; also when agreeing a rendezvous.

25 Grid references are usually quoted using **six figures**. The first three are the eastings; the second three are the northings. After quoting the grid reference, always describe the feature referred to, making it easier for the recipient to identify.

26 Sometimes references with just **four figures** are used as a rough guide to the area where a feature may be found (the first two are the eastings, the second two the northings).

27 Grid references are often **preceded by two letters** which also form part of the national grid system. However, these do not affect individual maps, and for most practical purposes need not be included. It is nowadays more common and practical to prefix the grid reference with the number of the appropriate Landranger sheet.

28 To **take the grid reference of a location on the map**, follow the procedure described in figure 3.

29 To **locate a point on the map from a given grid reference**, reverse the procedure described in figure 3.

Figure 3

To take a 6-figure grid reference

What is the grid reference of the church?

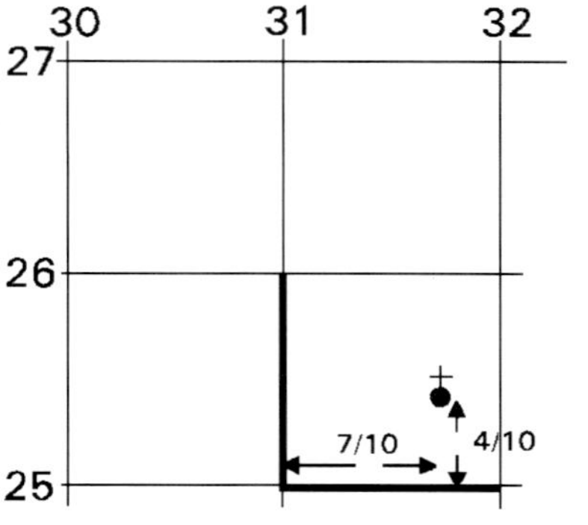

1. Identify the 1km square containing the church. Do this by selecting its left and bottom sides (imagine the letter "L" that bounds the square). Take the numbers on the edge of the map for these two sides (downstroke of the "L" first, just as you would write it). This gives:

   31_ 25_

   (Note One: 3125 is the 4-figure grid reference of the square)

   (Note Two: for ease of reading, the numbers against each grid line are repeated at 10km intervals in the body of the map)

2. Now an extra figure must be added to each pair of numbers to specify to the nearest 100m where the church lies within the square. Estimate the number of tenths (100m) the church lies from 'our' two sides, once again starting with the downstroke. How far from the downstroke? seven tenths. How far from the horizontal stroke? four tenths. Thus the 6-figure grid reference is:

   317 254

3. When quoting a grid reference, for confirmation and to guard against error, always say what the GR refers to:

   "the church at GR 317 254"

4. 6-figure grid references are repeated at 100km intervals across the country. If you need to define the GR uniquely, this can be done in either of two ways:

   Method 1. The 'correct' way is to identify the two-letter code allocated to the 100km square containing the church. Each 100km square covering the country has been allocated such a code and the one(s) referring to any particular map can be found from the map margin. In this example, say the code is 'SY', then the full grid reference is:

   "the church at GR SY 317 254"

   Method 2. A more informal but commonly used way of giving a unique grid reference is to quote the Landranger map sheet containing the location:

   "the church at GR Map 194/317 254"

30 Instructions for working out grid references are also **shown in the key** to Landranger and Outdoor Leisure maps.

31 A **romer** is useful for working out accurate 6-figure grid references, and for measuring short distances off the map directly in metres. It is a rectangular scale, marked with the figures 1 to 9, and can be found on many compasses. Separate plastic romers can also be obtained. Make certain to chose the correct romer for the scale of your map. Figure 4 demonstrates its use

Figure 4

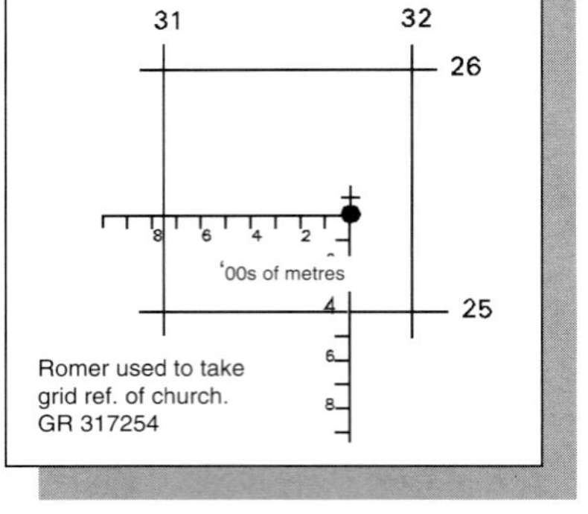

The compass

32 The compass is a navigational aid valued in all types of terrain by beginner and expert alike. However skilled map reading (see paragraphs 40 to 43 below) will always form the basis of good navigation, and the compass is no substitute for this. The compass should be regarded as a very useful, but not vital, additional tool.

A **compass** is an instrument for determining direction by reference to a freely turning magnetic needle. Figure 5 shows a basic compass. There are several different types, and you may wish to examine them in the shop to see which one suits you best. They are usually made of transparent plastic, and have two main parts: the *baseplate*; and the *housing*, which is rotatable.

Figure 5

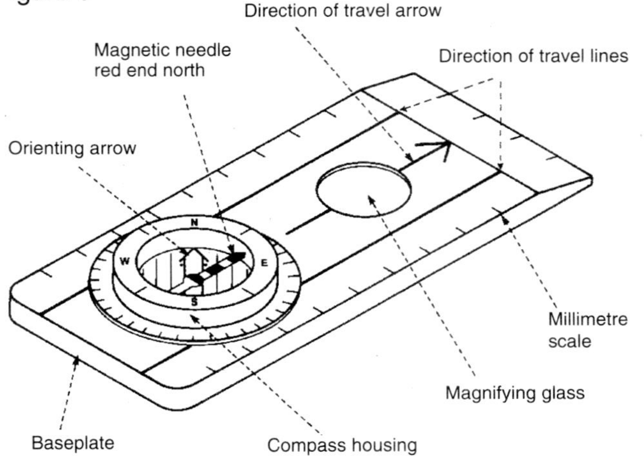

33 The compass needle points to **magnetic north**. For most walking purposes the difference between this and **grid north** is too small to worry about, but there are times when it is important (see box 8, page 28).

34 Grid lines on the OS maps actually point to **grid north**. The difference between this and true north can be ignored by walkers.

35 There are four main uses of the compass. The first is to **walk over open ground on a bearing** taken from the map (see figure 6). Here are some further hints and tips for walking on a bearing:

i If possible look for a distant feature lying on or close to the required direction of travel, such as a distinctive tree, a pylon, a church, or even a rock or a clump of grass. Then you need only to keep an eye on the feature, instead of having to check your compass frequently.

ii Over long distances, take every opportunity to re-confirm your direction on reaching a recognisable point, such as a field boundary, track, or stream.

iii When crossing open country, you may need to aim for a specific point on a linear feature such as a bridge over a

Figure 6

To walk on a bearing taken from the map

You wish to travel from your present position, Point A, to the trig point which you cannot see through the mist.

Step 1
Lay the compass on the map so that an edge of the baseplate (or one of the two direction of travel lines on the compass base) lies on the line of the required route. The direction of travel arrow must point in the direction you wish to go. (There is no need to set the map)

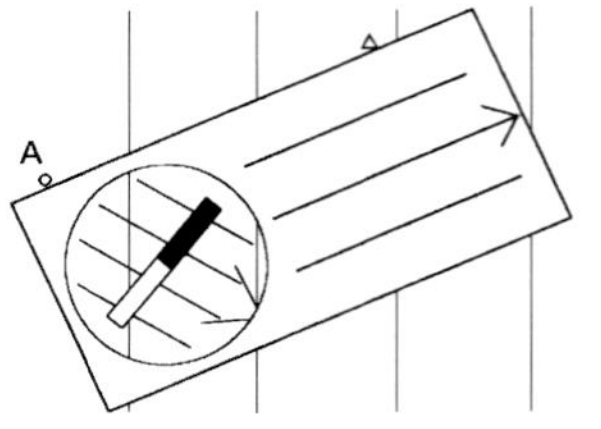

Step 2
Rotate the housing so that the orienting arrow points to north on the map and its lines lie parallel with the grid lines on the map. The figure on the rim of the housing at the direction of travel arrow is the bearing you will follow. (Ignore the magnetic needle while the compass is on the map)

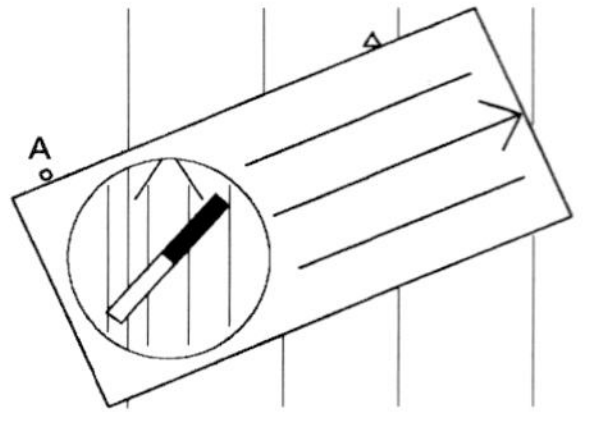

Step 3
Remove the compass from the map; hold it with the direction of travel arrow pointing directly away from you; then rotate your whole body, including the compass, until the red end of the magnetic needle lies parallel with the orienting arrow. The direction of travel arrow now points in the direction you should follow.

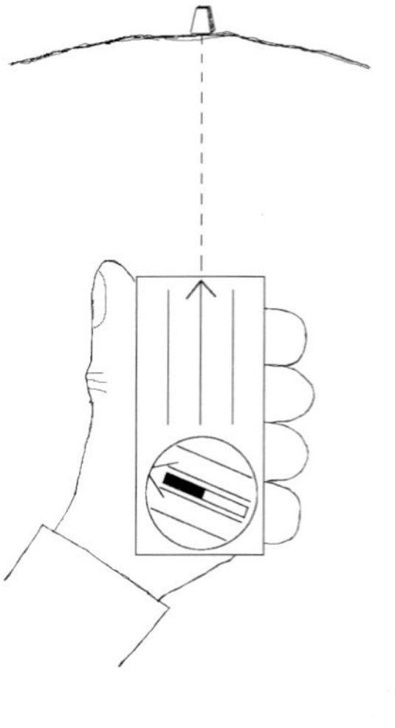

Step 4
If you have to follow a bearing over open ground and you cannot see your destination, sight along the direction of travel arrow and pick an object (e.g. a rock or bush) in the distance on this line. Put your compass away and walk to the object. Then repeat steps 3 and 4 until you reach your destination.

stream or the path entrance to a forest. If it is some distance away, you are unlikely to hit it spot on. It is then better to set a bearing for a point a couple of hundred metres to one side. Then, when you reach the linear feature but cannot see your target in the mist, you know whether to turn left or right to pick up the target. This technique is known as *aiming off*.

iv In some areas, especially woodland, paths frequently zigzag and it is impractical to take a bearing at every bend. To overcome this you can take the compass bearing across the wood from entry to exit and use this at path junctions, choosing the path nearest to the set bearing.

36 The second use is to **check the direction of a path** with its bearing taken from the map. To take the bearing of the path from the map, simply use steps 1 and 2 in figure 6 and use step 3 to check the path's direction on the ground.

Figure 7
Identifying a distant feature

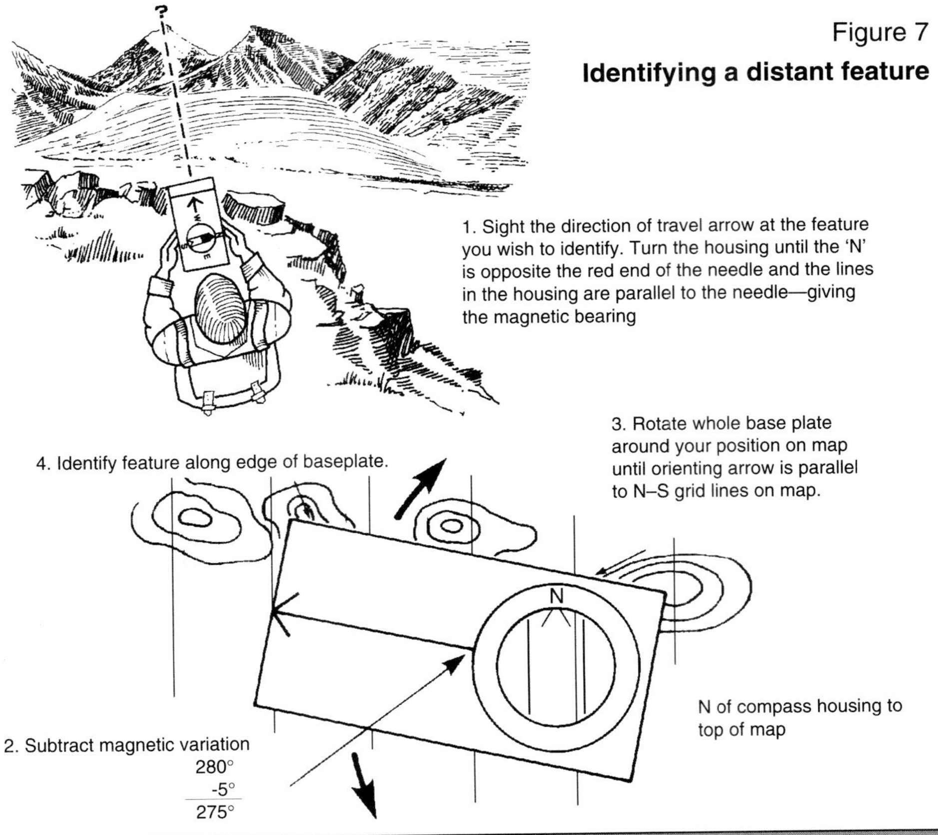

Box 8

Magnetic variation

It is perfectly acceptable to ignore magnetic variation when checking the bearing of a footpath or direction to travel over short distances (say, up to 1 km). However, for longer distances or where accuracy is needed, then magnetic variation should be allowed for. At a value of 5° west, to ignore magnetic variation gives rise to an error of about 10% of the distance travelled, to the left of the correct direction.

The complication comes from the fact that geographical and magnetic norths do not lie in the same place. Magnetic variation is the difference between the directions of magnetic north (the direction the magnetic needle points to) and grid north (the direction of the north-pointing grid lines on the map). Its value can be worked out from the information in the margin of the map. Currently (1993) it is always west of grid north but varies over the British Isles from 6.5° in East Anglia and NE Scotland to 3° at Land's End. What's more, it is decreasing by about a degree every 6 years. The 'average' 5° line now runs from the Isle of Wight, through the Lake District to the Isle of Skye.

Having worked out the value of magnetic variation for your map, you can choose one of two ways to apply it. (Let us assume it is 5°):

Method 1 (the usual method)
Having taken the grid bearing from the map (step 2 figure 6), convert it to a magnetic bearing by adding the variation. (e.g. bearing from the map = 167° magnetic bearing = 172°).
(Note: when working from ground to map – see paragraphs 37 and 38 – *subtract* magnetic variation to convert a magnetic bearing to a grid bearing).

Method 2
A 'permanent' and elegant modification to your compass saves having to do this sum. Using permanent (spirit-based) fine marker pens, draw a red line on the compass housing from the centre to the 355° mark and a blue line from the centre to the 175° mark (or whichever marks correspond to the magnetic variation for your map). Thereafter, when aligning the magnetic needle (i.e. using the compass off the map), use this new line instead of the orienting arrow. Magnetic variation is then automatically allowed for. (The line can be removed safely with methylated spirits).

37 The third use is to **identify distant features**. This is both useful, to help establish your direction of travel, and interesting, to give names to features you can see. Figure 7.

Figure 9 **Finding your location by resection**

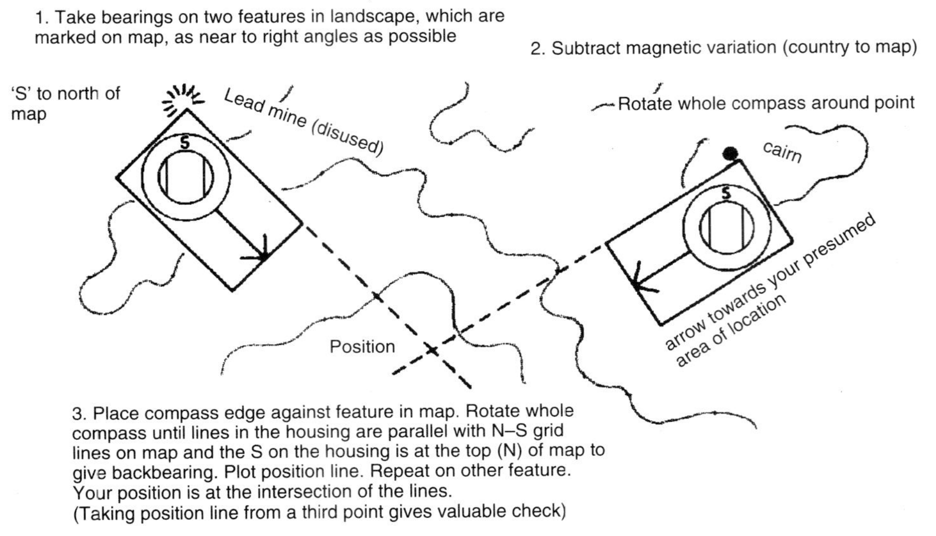

38 The fourth use is to **find your exact location**. For this you need at least two identifiable features in sight. See figure 9.

39 If you find it difficult at first to work with a compass, **don't give up!** It is true that many experienced leaders can navigate with minimal use of a compass by means of excellent map interpretation. However, whenever confidence is lacking, the compass provides an excellent check of direction, and when visibility is poor it could be essential. Thus it pays every walker to become proficient.

Beginners find that they quite quickly get the hang of using a compass, and then it becomes a very powerful help in map reading. You need to take about 10 to 15 bearings successfully to learn the technique thoroughly. Once learned, be sure to practice it on every walk for a time, so as not to forget.

Box 10

WARNING! The Three Big Compass Mistakes
Finding yourself pointing 180° in the wrong direction

When taking your bearing (figure 6), avoid:

Mistake 1 – do *not* put your compass on the map (step 1) with the direction of travel arrow pointing back to your present position!

Mistake 2 – do *not* rotate the housing (step 2) so that the orienting arrow points south on the map – or east or west!

Mistake 3 – do *not* rotate your body (step 3) so that the white end of the needle is aligned with the orienting arrow!

Relating map to countryside

40 Obviously, relating the map to the countryside (and vice versa) is a practical exercise which should be done in the countryside itself. However, it is possible to **visualise the countryside** whilst indoors through a close examination of the map. Start with the Pathfinder sheet that includes your home, even if the surroundings are urban, and work your way round your neighbourhood on the map, trying to recognise local landmarks.

41 At home, try **verbalising the map**, describing aloud what you expect to find from what appears on the map. This is best done with a companion.

42 After you have visualised the countryside from the map at home, go outside with your local Pathfinder sheet, to **relate the countryside to the map**. Work your way round the district and get used to the scale. See how the landmarks relate to what appears on the map. When you are accustomed to the "feel" of the map, you can venture further afield, using sheets for unfamiliar areas.

43 **Setting the map**, also called orientating the map, helps in relating map to countryside. This means turning the map so that your direction of travel is at the top. When this is done, all features are seen to lie in the same direction from your current position, both on the map and on the ground. Also, the north edge of the map points to north on the ground.

Not everyone needs or wishes to set the map, but it is a common and recommended practice – you must decide whether or not it will help you.

There are three basic ways of setting the map: by linear feature, by point feature, and by compass – see figures 11, 12 and 13.

Figure 11 **Setting the map by linear feature**

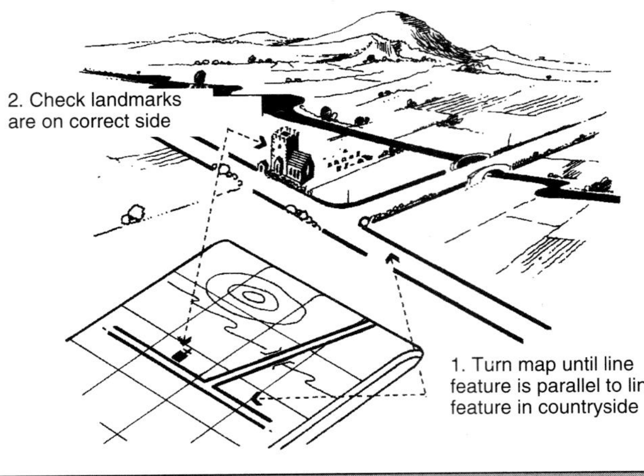

Figure 12 **Setting the map by point feature**

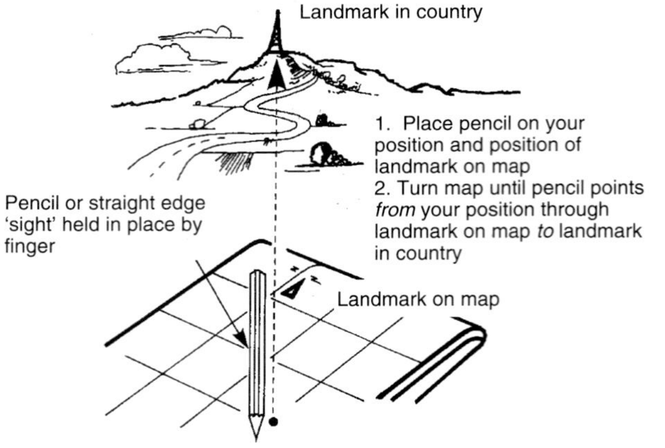

Figure 13 **Setting the map by compass**

Step 1
Place the compass anywhere on the horizontal map – you will be looking only at the compass needle

Step 2
Turn the whole map, including the compass, until the north–pointing grid lines are parallel with the needle, red end of needle pointing to north on the map

You can set the map by compass even if you cannot pinpoint your position on the map

Measuring distances

44 There are several ways of measuring distances, both for accuracy and as a rough guide. The methods described in paragraphs i to iv are best used at home when planning, for greater accuracy. Those in paragraphs v to viii are more useful while walking, as a rough guide.

i **Pencil in** your intended route, marking off each kilometre (or mile if preferred), and taking into account the twists and turns. This can be done most easily with a piece of thin string cut exactly to the scale equivalent of one kilometre (4 centimetres for 1:25,000 scale; 2 centimetres for 1:50,000 scale) or one mile (2.5 inches for 1:25,000; 1.25 inches for 1:50,000).

ii Cut a **piece of string** that is long enough to cover the whole of your intended route. Lay it along the route, again allowing for twists and turns. Then measure the total distance against the map scale.

iii Use one edge of a **sheet of paper** to mark off each straight section of your route – the whole route is then measured against the map scale.

iv Use a **map measurer** – a small gadget with a wheel that can be rolled along your route, the distance being indicated by a pointer moving against a scale. Some measurers have to be rolled back along the scale of the map until the pointer reaches its origin, again to measure the distance.

v Use **grid lines** on the map, which are exactly one kilometre apart, estimating by eye whilst making an allowance for the twist and turns of your route.

vi Use the **millimetre scale** on the edge of your compass. One millimetre represents:

25 metres	on	1:25,000 (Pathfinder map)
50 metres	on	1:50,000 (Landranger map)

vii On footpaths and bridleways, **count the dashes**. Each dash (together with its adjoining space), making up the red and green rights of way paths on Landranger and Pathfinder, represents a certain distance on the ground:

on footpath on	Pathfinder	it represents	30 metres
"	Landranger	"	50 "
on bridleway on	Pathfinder	"	70 "
"	Landranger	"	90 "

(this is the **30-50-70-90 Rule**)

viii Sometimes, when few mapped features can be seen in a forest or in mist, having obtained from the map a distance in metres to the next identifiable point, you may find it necessary to estimate this distance on the ground. For short distances of up to about 400 metres, use pacing; for longer distances, use timing. For both these methods, you must make allowances for steep slopes, muddy conditions underfoot, tiredness, and so on.

- For **pacing**, you need to know how many double paces you take over 100 metres, i.e. how often your left or right foot hits the ground (a person of average height might take 65 double paces). This can be done over a measured 100 metre length near your home. Then you can calculate the number of paces needed to cover the required distance, e.g. 195 double paces over 300 metres.
- For **timing**, you need to estimate your walking speed in kilometres per hour (kph) – again this can be done over a measured length near your home. Then you can work out how many minutes you need to allow for the distance to be travelled. At 4 kph (an average speed), it takes 1.5 minutes to cover 100 metres.

45 **Pedometers** can be used, but can also be very misleading in the countryside, because of the uneven paces taken in varying underfoot conditions.

Hints and tips

46 **Waymarks**. In many lowland areas you will find waymarks or signposts at intervals along the path. The waymarks usually take the form of an arrow, and it is standard practice to use yellow on footpaths, blue on bridleways. The arrows sometimes include the path number – useful if needing to report an obstruction (see paragraph 4.9).

47 **Guiding features**. When walking across a large field, or other open area, the exact point you need to aim for can often be gauged by taking note of another feature or landmark on the map, such as a church, that lies in the same direction. Or, when reconnoitring your walk, you can take note of a guiding feature which may not be identified on the map, such as a large tree, post or electricity pylon visible over the brow of a hill. You can often make out a stile or gate in the fence or hedge ahead. Binoculars can help to identify such small guiding features as stiles.

48 **Path usage**. The line of a path may be indicated in varying degrees, sometimes very faintly, by wear from the passage of previous users. This may just be scuff-marks in the grass from the boots of someone who only passed earlier on the same day, or footprints in the earth. Always check by map interpretation that they are leading in the required direction or by taking a compass bearing – they may have been made by the landowner following a different direction.

49 **Long distance view**. Before setting off on a new path, look ahead and check that distant features in your required direction tie up with what you are expecting.

50 **Counting bends**. Bends in the path show up very clearly while you are walking because of the foreshortening effect of viewing the path ahead from your own head height. This provides a valuable aid to navigation, constantly available and easy to use. For example, you might say, on reading the map, "from this bridge we look for the next path junction after a righthander, then a lefthander, then 200 metres".

51 **Keep in contact** with your map. At every opportunity, check that the features you encounter are what you

expected. In woodland, on a zigzag route with unmarked side paths, take frequent compass bearings to check that you are still heading in the right direction. If you come to a feature that you were not expecting, check your direction with a compass bearing. Bear in mind that the unexpected feature may not be marked on your map.

If you are unsure that the route you are following is correct, stop, take a compass bearing, and check that the surroundings appear correct. You should bear in mind that features on the map may have changed, for example a new wood may have been planted, or a hedge removed. With growing experience, you should develop a sixth sense that will nag away subconsciously, as a warning that you may be going wrong.

52 **Concentrate!** It is easy to be thinking about something else, or be talking to someone, and miss the point where you should take a turning.

53 **Ask advice**. Do not be afraid to ask experienced members of your party for a second opinion.

54 **Keep your head**. Do not let other members of your party rush you into following a direction until you are sure that it is the right one.

Global positioning system

55 The satellite technology mentioned in paragraph 21 above is the **global positioning system**, based on a number of satellites orbiting the earth at very high altitude. Information from these satellites can pinpoint positions anywhere in the world, 24 hours a day. There are already on the market a number of **global positioning receivers**, which not only give the user's exact location, but indicate the direction to be followed to reach a preset destination. At present, intended mainly for marine navigation, they are very expensive and have some technological limitations in situations encountered by walkers. However, in time, they are sure to become less expensive and, with improved technology, may well provide valuable help for walkers.

Practical exercises

Practical exercise 1 : **Exploring the map I**

Indoors. On a map, follow the shortest route from A to B, e.g. 'First take the track, fenced both sides, which rises gently while following the right-hand side of a valley and then climbs steeply. After that comes a walk along a ridge to its highest point, passing a number of knolls on the left, followed by a gentle descent along its northern shoulder'.

Practical exercise 2: **Exploring the map II**

Indoors. Choose your own routes on any map and follow them along, paying attention to fine detail, and describe the landforms you pass. Describe what you would see around at a point you are trying to pinpoint on the map.

Practical exercise 3: **Grid references**

Indoors. Choose five points on any Landranger, Pathfinder or Outdoor Leisure map and work out their grid references. Get someone to give you grid references from which to identify the locations referred to.

Practical exercise 4: **Verbalising the route**

Indoors. For any map, before using it outside, "verbalise the route" – that is, follow it on the map and describe what you will see. This may be easier if you work with a companion. Note the position of buildings, road and path turnings, woods, landforms etc.

Practical exercise 5: **Measuring distances**

Indoors. On a Pathfinder map, measure the shortest route between two points using paths and tracks, including rights of way where possible. Use as many as possible of the methods described in paragraph 44 above, and compare the distances obtained.

Practical exercise 6: **Compass bearings**

Indoors. On your planned route, work out on the map the compass bearings that you will follow all the way along it, and note them down in sequence in the following format:

1 From start 120° – 200 metres to path junction.

2 145° – 500 metres to road.

3 190° – 350 metres to church.

etc.

Check them when you walk the route.

Practical exercise 7: **Routefinding drill**

Outdoors. Divide your route into chunks, and verbalise each one as you come to its start, as in Exercise 4. Then as you walk through it for the first time, you can see whether your predictions turn out to be correct. Try memorising a short section of the route, then put the map away and follow it from memory – but first make sure that you are starting off in the right direction!

Practical exercise 8: **Permanent orienteering course**

Outdoors. Also known as wayfaring courses, these are primarily intended as an introduction to or training for orienteering, but give good practice for walkers since map and compass are used to locate a sequence of posts or signs placed at specific points in the woods. Their disadvantage is that the symbols used and the scale of the maps, usually 1:10,000 or 1:15,000, are different from those which are used for walking. The courses are usually devised and maintained by the local orienteering club, and located in large urban parks, country parks or forest parks. Details of their locations can be obtained from the British Orienteering Federation (see appendix 2 – National Navigation Award Scheme). The maps can be bought quite cheaply either from the orienteering club responsible, or from a nearby information or refreshment point.

Module 2: Planning your route

How to start

1 If you are planning to lead for an RA group or affiliated club, you should first **contact the events officer**, or whoever is responsible for putting together the programme of walks. He or she can advise on dates available in the calendar, suitable areas, what sort of distance to aim for, and perhaps even suggest a route and possible refreshment arrangements. Details of how to contact the appropriate officer should be shown in a programme or newsletter.

2 You may already have a general idea of the area in which you wish to plan a walk. Otherwise, there are several sources of ideas for routes that have been planned by others, and which can be amended if necessary to suit your own requirements. Such routes can help a new leader to gain experience and confidence before moving on to creating his or her own routes. Do not be ashamed to admit that your route has been taken or adapted from some other source – even experienced leaders sometimes do this. Such sources include:

i **Books and magazines** specialising in the outdoors (see appendix 1). Many of these include suggestions for walks of varying distances and in different parts of the country. They are usually tried and tested, and a full route description, including items of interest passed, is included. Make sure that the book or magazine has been recently published or re-issued.

ii In many areas, there is a network of named **long distance walking routes**, most of which have a guidebook or descriptive leaflet. Parts of them can be used for one-day walks, or they can be divided into sections for a series of walks over several weekends. Most of these routes are listed in the "Long Distance Walker's Handbook" (see appendix 1), but new ones are being created all the time. Bear in mind, though, that some well known routes are very popular and can be crowded at weekends and bank holidays.

iii Many **local authorities**, also parish and community councils, have set up walking routes within their areas. They are usually waymarked, and have descriptive leaflets which should be available at local libraries or tourist information centres.

3 For your **first attempt** at planning your own route, try to pick an area with which you are familiar. Do not be alarmed by the wide choice of possibilities, and remember that you cannot include all the suggestions given in this manual – at least not on one walk!

4 As for **choice of map scale for planning** a route, this is a matter of taste. Some prefer to work solely with the 1:25,000 scale, liking the accuracy and detail that can be read. Others prefer to work mainly with the 1:50,000 scale because the paths and contours show up better and the smaller scale enables a better overview of a route to be obtained. The 1:25,000 map is still needed to check out the detail of potential trouble spots.

Which routes to use

5 When planning your route, having decided on its basic format (circular or linear, preferably not out-and-back),

try to include as many as possible of these **desirable characteristics** of a walk:

- good views
- interesting villages, buildings or natural phenomena
- the right amount of steepness and climbing
- the right length
- a minimum of walking on busy roads
- some woodland, but not too much
- some waterside walking, but not too much
- a well timed lunch break in a pleasant place
- escape routes and shortening possibilities in case of need

6 In most areas there is a **wide choice** of route possibilities, using footpaths, bridleways, tracks, roads and open country.

7 Many of these routes are **rights of way**:

i Rights of way can include footpaths (accessible on foot only), bridleways (on foot, horseback or pedal cycle) and byways (usually wide unmetalled tracks or very minor roads accessible to all traffic including motor vehicles).

ii On Ordnance Survey maps covering England and Wales, rights of way are usually depicted in red or green. On OS maps covering Scotland, all paths are shown as black dashed lines – rights of way there are not shown.

iii Unless there is some technical reason for temporarily closing a right of way, for example a landslip or repairs, or a legal diversion or closure has been made (see paragraphs 4.24 to 4.26), the public has a right of access at all times. Unfortunately many of these routes are illegally obstructed at present – advice on what to do in these cases will be found in paragraphs 4.10 to 4.23.

iv Not all rights of way are indicated as such on OS maps covering England and Wales, and none of them are indicated on maps covering Scotland. In Scotland, far fewer rights of way have been secured, and many of these are only claimed as such by various interested parties, including walkers. There are established legal procedures for claiming a right of way. See the publications "Rights of Way: a guide to law and practice" and "Rights of Way: a guide to the law in Scotland", listed in appendix 1.

8 A **permissive path** (sometimes called a concessionary path) is one over which there is no legal right of way, but the owner of the land has given permission for the public to use it on foot, often through a formal agreement with the local authority. This sometimes applies to paths which are shown in black on OS maps – but not always. On some Outdoor Leisure maps, permissive paths are shown in brown. Such paths might not be shown on maps at all. The only ways to find out are by personal visit, or by enquiry to the local authority (see box 14). Use of such a path may be restricted to certain hours, days of the week or times of the year, and permission may be withdrawn without notice. A permissive path must be closed on one day every year, otherwise it may be claimed as a right of way.

Note: In this manual, for convenience, we generally use the word path to cover all rights of way and other footpaths.

9 A **public road** is maintained, usually by a local authority for use by the general public. On Landranger and Outdoor Leisure maps, most roads are shown in red, brown or yellow, according to their grade. Motorways are in blue, but of course walkers must not use them. On the Pathfinder maps these roads are all shown in brown. However, you should try to *avoid using roads* as much as possible, not only because they are more dangerous for walkers, but to maximise the use of footpaths and thereby help to keep them open.

10 On all OS Pathfinder, Landranger and Outdoor Leisure maps there are also routes known as **white roads**, because of their lack of colouring on the map.

i In urban areas, white roads are generally in residential or business districts, and are usually accessible to walkers, but some might be private estate roads.

ii In the country, white roads could be driveways leading to farms or houses, farm tracks or even old drove roads or ancient 'green lanes'.

iii If a white road is also a footpath or bridleway, the

appropriate red or green dashed line will also run along the line of the road in England and Wales (not in Scotland).

iv Where no right of way is shown, unfortunately the Ordnance Survey does not have the information to make clear whether such white roads exclude walkers – fortunately, most do not. The only sure ways of finding out are either by personal visit, or by contacting the appropriate local authority (see box 14).

11 Some privately owned land has either "formal" or "de facto" access. In many areas, **formal access** is provided by organisations or individuals who own land and have given specific commitments in favour of public access. These may be supported by legally binding arrangements or long standing traditions of dedication to public use. In such areas, freedom of access is usually encouraged across most of the land, except where conservation or management reasons require some restraint in particular locations.

Examples of places having formal access arrangements or traditions include:

- public parks
- country and regional parks
- some common land (England and Wales only)
- land owned by the Forestry Commission (Forest Enterprise), National Trusts, Woodland Trust
- most beaches, foreshore and coastline

In some areas, landowners have entered into formal access agreements with public authorities, and farmers are now taking up new grant aid schemes which make positive provision for public access, including the Countryside Stewardship Scheme.

Note: whilst much of the open land in **national parks** has some form of access, it should not be assumed that all land in national parks is accessible to the public.

12 In many areas, especially in Scotland, there is a recognition of **de facto access,** where landowners accept that there is a freedom of passage across their land. Such access is not protected in law at present, but walkers can usually expect

to enjoy unlimited access for most of the year. When landowners object to such access, and this might happen only at certain times, they are within their rights to ask walkers to leave their property.

13 On Ordnance Survey maps, only National Trust land is consistently indicated, and one can generally assume that there is unrestricted access to such areas bounded in red. However, at present, OS maps do not show consistently other access land, or their access points. Outdoor Leisure maps show some formal access land in national parks. Otherwise, the best way of finding out whether there is formal access, and where the access points are located, is either by visiting the land in question, or enquiring of the appropriate local authority (see box 14).

Box 14

Help from local authorities and other bodies

If you require information about access opportunities in an area, or if you encounter an obstruction or hazard on a path, the appropriate local authority may be able to help. The departments dealing with highways, recreation or planning (ask for the footpath officer) usually have various responsibilities relating to securing and encouraging public access in both town and countryside.

Local tourist information centres, or offices of the Countryside Commission, the Countryside Council for Wales, English Nature, the National Trust and Scottish Natural Heritage may also be helpful. Parish and community councils are often much involved with protecting public access opportunities close to villages and towns.

14 Avoid potentially **dangerous or difficult routes**, such as cliff edges or quarries with inadequate safety arrangements, or those where the path is obstructed in some way, e.g. missing bridges, heavily overgrown (see module 4

– Trouble-shooting). If use of such routes is unavoidable, ensure that the more experienced members of your party are ready to assist the less confident ones when necessary.

15 When planning your route, try to avoid any unnecessary **conflict with conservation interests**, or other recreational users, or land management interests. Equally important, though, is the need to uphold the traditional uses and rights that have been secured by walkers over many years.

How long should the walk be?

16 If you are leading for an RA group or affiliated club, you should first discuss with the **events officer** what sort of distance is suitable, though of course your own preferences must be taken into account.

17 A **half day walk** taking place in the morning, afternoon or on a summer evening could be anything up to 10 kilometres (6 miles).

18 A **whole day walk** during British Summer Time could be anything from 16 to 24 kilometres (10 to 15 miles), or even more, depending on the starting and finishing times and how far you have to travel to the area. In winter, shorter days will probably limit a whole day walk to 11 to 16 kilometres (7 to 10 miles).

Timing the walk

19 The **average walking speed** of a party of more than 3 or 4 people should generally be reckoned at about 3 kilometres (2 miles) per hour, including time for a couple of short refreshment stops. Individuals and parties of less than 3 or 4 people may go at a faster pace, depending on their capabilities.

20 Some walkers enjoy a **fast pace**. They can be catered for, but this should be made clear in the programme, to deter slower walkers. Even so, it is unlikely that the speed will rise to much more than about 5 kilometres (3 miles) per hour overall.

21 Other walkers prefer a **gentle pace**, averaging perhaps 2 kilometres an hour. Every walk programme should offer walks at this pace, which should be advertised as such.

22 You may need to **allow more time** if:

i The party is large (more than 20 people), because the members are likely to spread out more, and your catching up stops will last longer.

ii There are lots of obstacles such as stiles and kissing-gates to negotiate – you may need to allow two or three minutes extra for each one.

iii Your route involves a considerable amount of height gain. Allow 30 minutes extra for every 300 metres of ascent.

iv You intend to spend an hour or so at a pub for lunch.

v You intend to make a number of stops to point out items of interest.

vi Your walk is open to families with pushchairs.

Adding interest

23 Make your route as interesting as possible by including **points of interest**, such as churches, photogenic villages, historic buildings, ancient monuments, stately homes, country parks, nature reserves etc. The area may be

associated with a historical person or event, or with a theme such as a medieval industry.

24 Assess your route for the **quality of its views**. Many good viewpoints are marked on OS maps, but since these are often aimed at motorists, interpretation of the contours is usually a better guide for walkers. If possible, do not stay in flat terrain all the time, unless you expect a party of less able-bodied members. Include a variety of landscapes, and do not stay for too long in woodland where views are restricted or absent.

25 Most people like to walk beside **water**, and it is often possible to include a coastal, lakeside or riverside path, or a canal towpath.

26 More enjoyment will be added if some **activity** is likely, such as at a canal lock, a steam railway station, a working windmill or waterwheel.

27 Allow time for **photographs**, but do not let the keen photographers delay the party for too long.

28 Try to obtain some **information** about the places you will pass – a local library or tourist information centre should be able to help – and tell your party what you know. Be prepared for supplementary questions – if necessary make it clear that you are not an expert.

29 Some party members will be interested in the **wildlife** that you see. If you have any knowledge, be prepared to pass it on. If not, ask on the day if any party member is knowledgeable about wildlife, and ask them to help.

30 Unless a special interest is the theme of your walk, **do not overdo the interest stops**. Your party members have probably come mainly to walk, and may get impatient with too many long stops.

31 If there is time, and it does not take too long, you could include a **visit to a place of interest.** Some provide welcome facilities such as refreshments and toilets. Make sure that the visit is mentioned in the group or club programme, and again at the start of your walk. Say if an admission fee is payable (avoid expensive places), how long the visit will

last, and stress that it is optional.

If the property to be visited is run by an organisation whose members qualify for free admission (e.g. English Heritage, Historic Scotland, Welsh Historic Monuments, National Trust, National Trust for Scotland) this should be mentioned, so that walkers know to bring their membership cards.

32 If you are expecting a sizeable number of **children**, try to maintain their interest with something to do during the walk. For example:

- a quiz from things to be spotted along the way
- a scavenger hunt of things that they can collect (but without causing damage to property or wildlife)
- matching colours of things seen along the route with those in their clothing

---

Transport arrangements

33 It is **RA policy** to encourage the use of public transport to reach walking areas, though it is appreciated that this is impractical in some parts of the country. On Sundays in particular, some rural bus and train services do not operate, and some intermediate railway stations may be closed.

A compromise can sometimes be reached by using public transport to a nearby point, then arranging for members with cars to ferry other party members to and from the walk.

34 Hire of a **coach or minibus** by your group or club may be feasible if a minimum number of participants can be guaranteed – sometimes by offering more than one walk. This also provides opportunities for linear routes.

35 If **public transport** is available:

i Check the time of a suitable outward bus or train. The departure time from a convenient stop or station in your area should be published in your group or club programme. Most programmes advise members to check bus and train times nearer the date, as they are subject to alteration.

ii For a linear walk using trains, check that the ticket is valid from the return station. This may not be the case if it is on a different line; in these circumstances it may be advantageous to book a ticket to a more distant station in order to gain the benefit of a return ticket, and if so it should be mentioned in the programme.

iii Check the times of return buses or trains, and allow a reasonable safety margin to cover possible delays in reaching the finishing point. Avoid if possible aiming to catch the last bus or train – have at least one in reserve.

iv Walks using public transport may also be made accessible to car passengers if required, in which case a meeting time at the destination should be published in the programme. If the route is linear, check that it is possible for drivers to return to their cars.

36 If **cars** are to be used:

i Decide on a convenient meeting point and time, which will be published in the programme, together with the grid reference.

ii Check that there are adequate parking facilities at the starting point. This should if possible be an official car park – if a charge is made, mention it in the programme. Avoid places where several parked vehicles may cause inconvenience to residents or businesses, or to churchgoers on Sunday mornings.

iii It is sometimes possible by agreement with the proprietor to leave vehicles in the car park of a pub or cafe, provided that it is patronised by your party at some stage during the day.

Refreshments and toilets

37 All except very short walks should have breaks for refreshments at some stage, and the group or club programme should inform members what they are.

38 For **refreshments**, it is generally the leader's decision to have a picnic stop, or to visit a pub or tea-room. However, some groups or clubs may have a policy in this respect, so the leader should discuss this with the appropriate officer.

39 Many walkers prefer to **picnic**, enjoying the sense of freedom and the fresh air, and it is less expensive. If it is intended to have a picnic lunch, or no refreshment facilities are available, members should be advised in the programme to bring their own food and drink.

40 Other walkers particularly enjoy visiting **pubs**, where the toilet facilities are in any case appreciated by everyone. There are two schools of thought about pubs: some love them, others hate them or are indifferent. You may have both types in your party.

If a pub stop is included in your walk, it should last about 45 to 60 minutes. This gives time for 'pub-lovers' to have a couple of drinks and some food, while 'pub-haters' can have a quick drink and visit the toilets, or sit outside and eat their own food without having to wait too long for the others. Remember that many pubs are happy to provide coffee and tea. Try to find a pub in a village which is interesting enough for 'pub-haters' to explore while waiting.

Usually, pubs will be happy to accept a party on the understanding that its members will buy drinks there. Many pubs are used to catering for large numbers of bar meals and snacks, so special arrangements for food may not be necessary. It is not normally practicable to make special catering arrangements for walk parties, as the pub will probably require a guarantee of the amount of food that will be bought, and this cannot usually be given.

A pub will normally only agree to party members eating their **own food** on the premises if it does not itself provide food. In any case, always ask if there is any objection to consumption of own food.

If **children** are expected on your walk, check whether the pub will admit them – it may have a family room. Children are usually allowed if there is a garden, but check the pub's wet/cold weather policy.

41 In much-visited locations, **temporary refreshment facilities** such as kiosks or vans may be available, especially at weekends.

42 When **reconnoitring** your route (see paragraph 50 below), take note of any refreshment facilities, such as pubs, cafes or tea-rooms, together with their opening and closing times and a telephone number.

43 If you decide to include stops at any of these places, call in or telephone to check that the manager or proprietor **welcomes walking parties**. They will need an idea of the approximate number and arrival time.

If there are several establishments close together, it may not be necessary to give advance warning: the party members can divide and choose between them.

44 Inevitably, **toilet facilities** will be required at some stage during your walk. Make a note of any permanent public facilities along or near the route. If you are intending to visit a pub for lunch, it will have toilets. Look out for places in the woods or behind bushes which may be suitable for "alfresco toilets".

Other considerations

45 **Circular v linear**. When public transport or a hired coach or minibus is used, both options are equally practical, though it can be more satisfactory to opt for a linear route (starting and finishing at different points), as this allows a wider coverage of the area.

When cars are used, a circular route is usually the only satisfactory option. It may be possible to leave one car at the start and another at the finish, but this is a cumbersome process. Public transport may help to get from one end to the other – if so, it is better to use it at the start, to remove the worry about a missed connection.

Figures 15 and 16 show examples of typical linear and circular routes. Limitations of space dictate use of the 1:50,000 Landranger maps here.

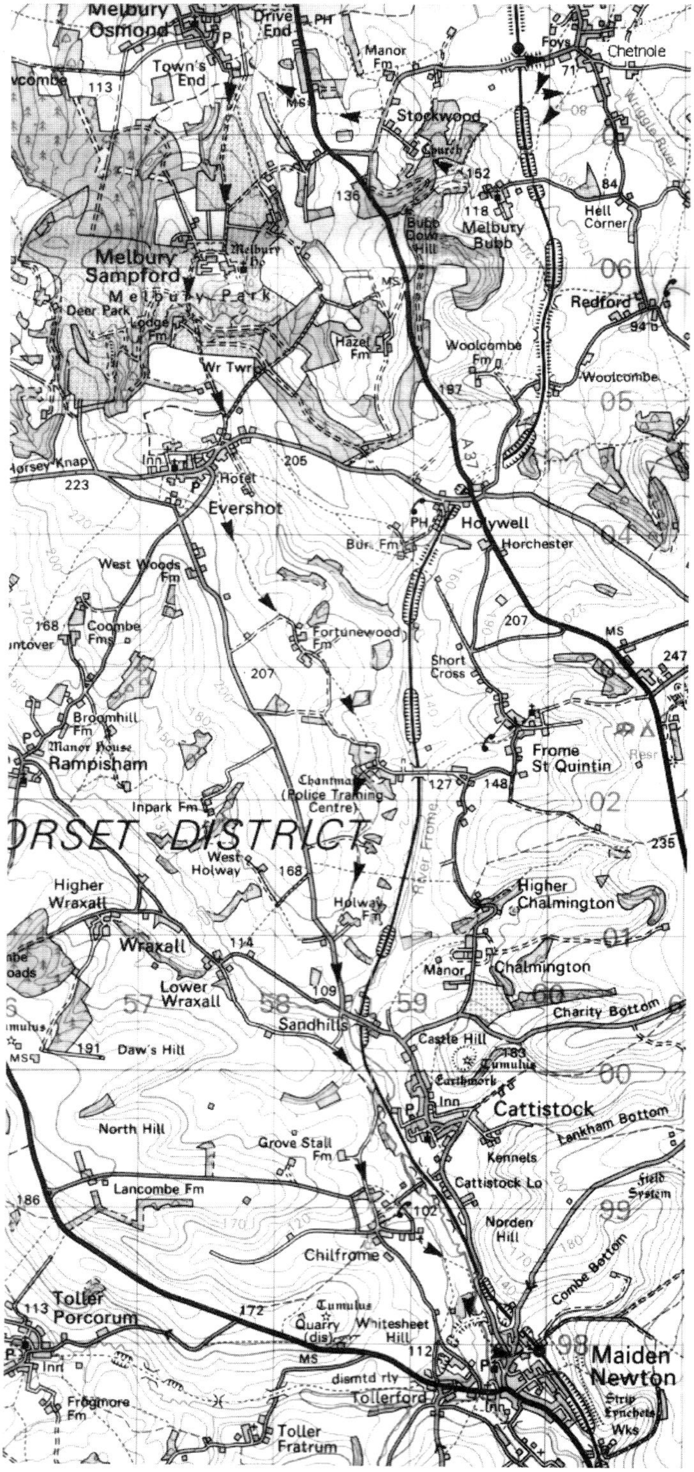

Figure 15

Maps: Landranger 194 Dorchester, Weymouth and surrounding area, and/or Pathfinders 1298 (ST40/50) Crewkerne and Beaminster and 1317 (SY49/59) Bridport.

(map scale reduced by 10%)

Figure 15 (cont.)

You have discovered that the trains run conveniently between Chetnole and Maiden Newton in this pleasant part of West Dorset. At the end of the walk, car drivers can take the train with the party back to the starting point.

Planning to start at Chetnole, after quite a lot of fiddling about, you decide on the route indicated on the map extract. This has the following features:

- Distance: 14.5 km long (9 miles), 250 m. of climbing (800 feet)
- Walk duration: at a speed of 4 km (2.5 miles) an hour, allow 3 hr. 35 min, plus 25 min. for the climbing, plus 20 min. for breaks and 45 min. for lunch = 5hr. 5 min. total.
- Lunch break at Evershot, which appears from the map to be well endowed with hostelries, conveniently after 7 km (4.5 miles) from the start.
- Only one kilometre of road work and that along minor roads.
- Option to extend the route after lunch by going through Frome St Quintin (see map) and rejoining the original route at Sandhills - making the total route 17.5 km. long (11 miles) with 410 m. of climbing (1300 feet). This option would have to be decided on beforehand and the route advertised in its longer form.

Specific route design points:

- From Chetnole station, visit Melbury Bubb (looks interesting) before climbing to nearby trig. point (views).
- Then go NW via Stockwood to be able to make a nearly direct crossing of the busy A37.
- Stretch through Melbury park might be tarmacked, but track is shown as unfenced, so grassland walking should be possible. Melbury House looks interesting.
- Paths go clearly S from Evershot to Sandhills; then there is a short stretch along a non-right of way path, plus white roads. It's deep Dorset, so they should be OK (ie. no 'private' signs), but if private, take road via Cattistock to Chilfrome.
- Nice-looking riverside path from Chilfrome to Maiden Newton, but we cannot be sure that a footbridge across the River Frome exists (it's marked only as a 'single line' stream here and the Landranger map does not show footbridges over these. The Pathfinder map marks them as "FB"). The disused rail bridge nearby might be pressed into use if there is no footbridge. This and the previous point need to be checked out on the reconnaissance walk, if an organised ramble is intended. Also check that all the paths are open.

(Note. The idea of taking a route further east was examined, but the paths did not connect up well and some unpleasant walking along the A37 was needed).

Programme notice:

11 June 9 miles 10.32	Linear walk from Chetnole to Maiden Newton. Rather hilly ramble visiting three churches and the village of Evershot (pub lunch or picnic) Meet Chetnole station 10.32 (Yeovil 10.12 Dorchester 9.47) Car drivers can take train back to starting point Leader: Abraham Smith (Tel: 088-997755)

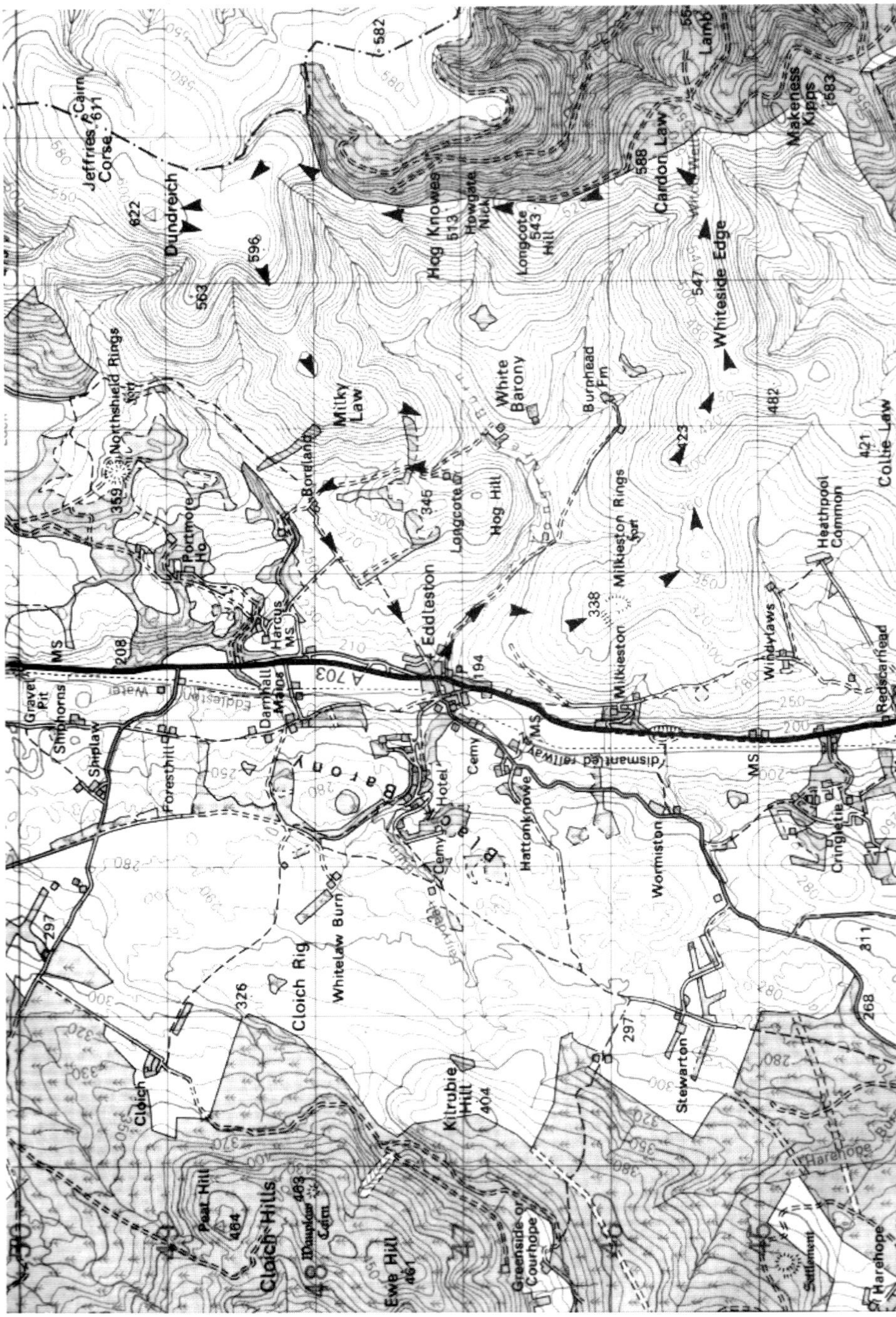

Figure 16

Maps: Landranger 73 Peebles, Galashiels & surrounding area, and/or Pathfinder 448 (NT24/34) Peebles.

Figure 16 (cont.)

Eddlestone, less than 20 miles S of Edinburgh on the Peebles road, looks to be a likely centre for a fine walk. The Moorfoot hills to the east provide the key. Looking closely at the map, a classic 'horseshoe' route is revealed, where you ascend into the hills by one spur, walk a ridge and then descend by the next spur.

Our route, marked on the map extract, ascends Whiteside Edge to Cardon Law, follows the narrow ridge to the N via a number of lesser hills, and culminates at Dundreich (just over 2000 feet). All-round views should be fabulous all the way, given clear weather. It looks as though the forest to the E stops just short of the crest of the ridge and should therefore not obscure the views. Anyway, it lies alongside the route only for just over a mile.

The main part of the route lies on open ground with no paths marked. Local knowledge dictates that the vegetation is likely to be rough grass, easy enough to walk over. The reconnaissance walk (or a look at the Pathfinder map) will determine whether there are any fences or walls to cross; probably few or none.

Detailed aspects of the walk:

- Distance: 13 km (8 miles), height gain about 600m (2000 feet, say).
- Walk duration calculation: assume 3.5 km an hour as much of the walking goes over rough grass, so allow 3 hr. 40 min. for the distance. Add 60 min. for the height gain. Add 1 hr 15 min. for stops and lunch. Say, 6 hrs. altogether, plus 30 mins for contingency.
- Route is nowhere too steep for comfort in ascent or descent (as is often the case when walking along spurs and ridges). No rocky places.
- In the event of weather turning nasty, could escape from Longcote Hill down spur to the square wood and thence to White Barony.
- A bad weather retreat from Dundreich looks easy enough to navigate on the spur along which the indicated route runs, via Milky Law.
- In the event of low cloud making a high route unappetising, there are a number of low level route possibilities to the west of Eddlestone - to Greenside Courhope, for example.

Programme notice:

11 July 8 miles 10.00	Circular hill walk over some fine trackless tops in the Moorfoot hills, ascending Cardon Law and Dundreich. Grassy, easy underfoot 2000 feet of ascent. Low level alternative if the weather's v. bad Meet10.00 am: at the post office, Eddlestone (GR Map73/243471) Leader: Alastair McShane (Tel: 099-887766)

46 **Which way round?** Study the map to see whether there are any advantages or disadvantages. For example, a steep and slippery hill may be more easily tackled upwards. Consider how your choice of lunch and tea stops will be affected by your expected time of arrival. On a linear route, you may be able to avoid some climbing by starting at the higher point, or the timings of public transport may be better at one end in the morning or afternoon.

47 **Time of year**. Choose terrain that is suitable for the time of year. Some routes may be subject to adverse conditions in winter – for example: cliff paths are dangerous in icy conditions and strong winds; stepping stones across a river may be under water; bus or train services may not operate; a major event may make the area and its facilities crowded – this can be checked by contacting the local tourist information centre.

48 **Conditions underfoot.** At any time of year, certain paths can be so muddy or slippery as to make progress slow, uncomfortable or even hazardous. This particularly affects bridleways and byways, which in wet weather are liable to be churned up by horses and vehicles. In shaded areas, such paths can stay muddy even in long dry periods. Try to avoid them if they are likely to be affected in this way – your reconnaissance (see below) will help to identify them. If use of such a path is unavoidable, warn your party about the conditions, apologise for them, and be prepared to help the less able-bodied get through the worst parts.

49 **Sense of achievement**. Walkers usually enjoy their day out more if they feel they have achieved something. This will depend on the individual, for example: the first time to have walked ten miles; a visit to a beauty spot which is inaccessible by car; visiting a place of interest; reaching a hill-top or ridge after a strenuous climb. The more opportunities of this kind that can be included in your route, the more satisfied your party members will be.

Reconnaissance

50 When you have decided on your route, you should always try to carry out a **reconnaissance** – sometimes called a reccy

or recce, survey, walk-out or try-out. If you are leading an RA walk on which members of the public are invited, a reconnaissance must be done.

51 A reconnaissance will **familiarise** you with turnings along the way, and make you seem more competent to your party. It is much easier, and less embarrassing, to sort out difficulties beforehand on your own, rather than with a party breathing down your neck! A reconnaissance lets you:

i Check that the paths you intend to use are clear of obstructions, and identify alternative routes in case of need.

ii Check whether any paths have been officially closed or diverted since your copy of the map was published.

iii Learn the route to ensure effortless navigation on the day. This can include noting things to look out for that indicate an approaching turn, or act as a guideline to an out-of-sight target.

iv Spot ways of improving the route that may not be apparent on the map – for example, a new path which cuts out a stretch of road-walking.

v Investigate possibilities for refreshment and toilet stops.

vi Investigate places of interest, and anticipate questions about them from party members.

vii Check your anticipated timings at suitable points along the route.

viii Consider escape routes in case of bad weather or unforeseen circumstances.

52 Do **report obstructions or difficulties** found during the reconnaissance. You may even be able to have them removed before the day of the walk. (See Module 4 paragraph 9).

53 If your reconnaissance took place some time ago, you may wish to check it again a short period before the day of your walk, as **circumstances may have changed** in the meantime.

54 If possible, the reconnaissance should be undertaken together with your **backmarker**, or rearguard. This will:

i Provide some company during your reconnaissance – and two pairs of eyes are better than one.

ii Make it easier for him or her to take over as leader if you are unable to attend for any reason.

iii Help the backmarker to take a turn in leading some parts of the walk on the day – this is also a way of training new leaders.

Recording your route

55 You should **record your route** in some way. This helps you to remember it on the day, and provides a means of noting points of interest, suitable places for refreshments, and so on. We suggest one of the following methods:

i A route card (see paragraph 56).

ii Marking it in pencil on your map.

iii Taking a photocopy of the appropriate map section, and marking the route on that. This method also easily allows you to mark places of interest, expected times of arrival, difficulties and so on. The Ordnance Survey say that they have no objection to this, provided that just one copy is taken. If you intend to distribute several copies, you must obtain their consent – see paragraph 6.12.

56 A **route card** is a helpful reminder to follow on the day. In certain circumstances, you may wish to leave a copy with a responsible person who is not coming on your walk (such as a relative, or a group or club officer) for use in the event of an accident or emergency – make sure to inform them when you have returned safely.

The route card should include, in the order in which you reach them (together with grid references where appropriate):

i Starting point and meeting time.

ii Main turnings and places passed, together with distances

between them, estimated times of arrival, and directions to be taken (in the form of points of the compass or bearings as preferred).

iii Notes of potential difficulties and alternative routes if needed.

iv Refreshment and toilet facilities.

v Finishing point and estimated time of arrival.

Figure 17 shows an example of a typical route card.

57 After your reconnaissance, do not assume that your route is now perfect, as you may still be able to find **further improvements**.

Figure 17

ROUTE CARD (Use one per day)

Day of the week: TUES | Date: 7TH JULY 1989 | Day of Venture 1st, 2nd etc:

NAMES OF GROUP MEMBERS: BARBARA MAIDMENT, MARTYN COX, PAUL RUSSELL, SUE SMITH, ELEANOR HANSON, MILFORD HINDMAN.

NAME OF GROUP OR UNIT: FOCUS YOUTH CLUB

ADDRESS: RAILWAY APPROACH HANWORTH.

TEL. No. 019-375-205

Setting out time: 9.00 am.

Leg	PLACE WITH GRID REF	General Direction or bearing	Distance in km/~~miles~~	Height climbed in m/~~ft~~	Time allowed for leg	Time for stops or meals	Total time for leg	Estimated Time of Arrival E.T.A.	Details of route to be followed	Escape to:
	START SELSIDE 783795									
1	TO PATH JCT SULBER 777735	SW then S	2·8	80	50	10	60	10·00	Walled path towards Alum Pot then Gillgarth Beck, then path S to Sulber.	Return.
2	TO SHOOTING HUT 766739	W	1·3	50	25	10	35	10·35	Follow path by Sulber and Nick Pots, then by wall.	E to Horton.
3	TO INGLEBOROUGH 741745	W	2·9	300	85	30	1·55	12·30	Path to Allotment Wall then across Simon Fell Breast to summit.	Return.
4	TO LITTLE INGLEBOROUGH 743735	E then S	1·4	–	20	10	30	13·00	Retrace path to Swine Tail then follow path towards Cairn.	Return by same route.
5	TO SWALLOW HOLE GREY WIFE SIKE 737723	between S and SW	1·4	–	20	10	30	13·30	Take SW fork at Junction with Gaping Gill path.	South by same path.
6	TO NEWBY COTE 732705	between S and SW	1·9	–	30	–	30	14·00	Follow path or Sike bed.	South by same path.
7	TO								ALTERNATIVE ROUTE FOR BAD WEATHER. Follow proposed route to Sulber	then path to
8	TO								Trow Gill, then Long Lane to then Old Road to Newby Cote.	Clapham and
	Totals		11·7 km	430m	3hr 50	1hr 10	5hrs	14·00	Supervisor's Name, Location, Tel No. EUAN FERGESON, PETER PARFREY, INGLETON YOUTH HOSTEL. 93-75205.	

Publicising your walk

58 Normally, for walks organised **only for members** of RA groups and affiliated clubs, a leader would not be involved in advance publicity, as a mention in the **programme or newsletter** is all that is needed.

59 If your walk is to be made **available to the public**, there are further considerations to be taken into account, and these are covered in module 5.

60 However, it is the leader's responsibility to **provide all the required information** to the programme editor in time for publication. Depending on the closing date, it may not be possible to give more than basic details. However the very least that will be required are:

Date, day of the week, starting point, meeting time, approximate walking distance, an idea of the terrain (hilly, level etc.), whether lunch will be a picnic or at a pub; plus, as appropriate, the departure time from a convenient point of a connecting bus or train, or the location of car parking facilities.

If possible, also include the main points of interest. State the walking pace to be taken by the group. The more information you can put in the programme, the more you are likely to attract the people for whom the walk is most suitable.

Practical exercises

Practical exercise 9: **Planning drill**

Indoors.

1. Choose your walk area, or highlight the main point to visit.
2. Decide the basic format of the walk (circular v linear, public transport or not, length, timings, amount of climbing).
3. Look over the chosen area for pleasant stretches of path.
4. Form a possible route by stringing stretches together.
5. Assess the route against your objectives and the criteria outlined earlier in this module.
6. Adjust the route as necessary to meet these objectives as far as possible.
7. Repeat stages 5 and 6 until you are satisfied that your route is as good as you can make it.

Practical exercise 10: **Planning routes**

Indoors. Plan a number of routes to meet the following objectives, and work out the expected walking times. No more than a quarter of the route should be on roads, and none on A or B roads.

1. One that is circular from a car park; 5 kilometres long; includes a stretch beside water; visits a building of interest.
2. One that is linear, between railway stations; 14 kilometres long; no more than 300 metres of climbing in total; visits a village with a pub for lunch.
3. One that is circular from a car park; 20 kilometres long; visits the highest hill-top within reach (but not a mountain); has a picnic lunch stop.

Practical exercise 11: **Route card**

Indoors. Work out a short route on any map, then compile an imaginary route card of what you would expect to find.

SECTION B: LEADERSHIP

Module 3 : On the day of your walk

Before leaving home

1 Take note of the **weather forecast** on the morning of your walk, and indeed a day or two beforehand, as well as the **travel news**. If developments may affect your walk, or how people may travel to it, consider any action you can take to alleviate the problems (see paragraphs 4.37 and 4.42).

At the meeting point

2 If you have not already got one, appoint a **backmarker** (see paragraph 2.54, also paragraph 18 below) from the party members. This should preferably be an experienced walker who can map-read. If he or she did not reconnoitre the route with you, give a short briefing on the route.

3 It is important to **talk to the party** before setting off. Do not just turn on your heel and go, as this gives a bad impression. You may prefer to stand on a high vantage point, if available, to make yourself more easily seen and heard. There are several things to say, and these are mentioned below. Keep your talk informal – try not to make it sound like a speech.

4 Some leaders find it helpful to prepare an **information sheet** which serves as an aide-memoire to things to say at the meeting point, and can also be distributed to the party members if so desired. However, this should not be considered as a substitute for talking.

5 Here are the basic things to say before setting off:

i First of all, **welcome** the party members.

ii **Introduce yourself** as the leader, and then introduce the backmarker.

iii Briefly **describe the route** by mentioning its distance, refreshment breaks, toilet facilities and any outstanding items of interest. Use the map to point out the route.

iv State the expected **finishing time**, pointing out that this might be subject to delay.

v Ask party members **not to walk in front of the leader** unless otherwise instructed (see also paragraph 17 below).

vi Ask everyone to make sure that the **person behind is in sight** when turning on to a new path, and say that, if anyone loses touch with the rest of the party, they should return to the last turning point (see paragraph 4.44).

vii Say that people should **feel free to stop** the party briefly for any minor emergency, particularly to remove a stone from a boot or to adjust footwear.

viii Say that, if anyone thinks that they may have **difficulty in completing the walk**, they should have a quiet word with you before setting off. (This allows anyone with a medical problem to bring it to the leader's attention in private).

ix If there are any **toilet facilities** at or near the start, point them out and say how long it will be to the next ones.

x Ask if anyone has **any questions**.

6 If anyone asks about **leaving en-route**, tell them what the possibilities are. Ask them to let you know if and when they decide to leave the party. Do not raise this subject yourself – it is not something to be encouraged. See also paragraph 4.45.

7 Check to see that everyone appears **suitably attired** for the expected terrain and weather conditions, and seems **physically capable** of handling them. Of course, you and the backmarker should also wear suitable gear to set a good example. For advice on what to do if anyone is obviously grossly ill-prepared or ill-suited, see paragraph 4.43.

8 If there is anyone with an apparent **disability**, such as being deaf, blind or partially sighted, make sure that they are kept informed and aware of any instructions and items of interest. If help is needed, offer it discreetly. It is unlikely that a blind or partially sighted person would come along unaccompanied, but if this happens, make sure that a

sighted person accompanies him or her during the walk. People in wheelchairs are unlikely to come unless the walk has been specially vetted for accessibility, and advertised as such.

9 **Unaccompanied children** should not be accepted on your party unless you have the written consent of a parent or guardian. However if any turn up unexpectedly, you cannot send them away unless you are near their home, or there is someone to look after them. You will then need to keep a special eye on them, and check that they are accounted for at each rest and refreshment stop, and at the finish.

10 Most RA groups and affiliated clubs have a policy regarding **dogs** being permitted on their walks, which the leader should enforce. If any party member has one, check that it is on a lead, and point out that it must be kept on its lead on roads and in fields with livestock and where the terrain requires careful footwork. See also paragraph 24 below.

12 If **cars** were used for transport to the start, check that they have been parked responsibly (see paragraph 2.36), advising people to move their cars if necessary. For security, warn car passengers not to leave valuables in the car, nor to leave notes which suggest that they will be away all day, or show their address.

13 For the benefit of **latecomers**, if practicable, leave a note of the location of your lunch stop at the start, and how to reach it. This is usually only possible at railway stations, where details can be left at the booking office, or at official car parks, if there is a notice board (but not on cars – see paragraph 12 above).

14 **Count the number** of people. With a large party, or if starting at a busy railway station, it may be more practicable to do this at a quieter point soon after the start – if possible choose a narrow point such as a gate where people must go in single file. It is sometimes better to ask the backmarker to do the counting, as he or she will have less to do at the start.

15 If you have made **special arrangements for catering** at your lunch or tea stop, you may need to ask at the start how many people wish to take advantage of them, and then telephone

the establishment to confirm the number. Again this is something for the backmarker to do.

16 Before setting off, many leaders make a **list of names** of their party members – this helps them to remember names, it may be of use in an emergency, and can even sometimes be used as evidence of use of a footpath.

During the walk

17 It is the general rule that **the leader should be at the front** of the party, and party members should be asked not to walk ahead. However, this does not prevent the leader from dropping back from time to time, in order to speak to party members, or encourage the slower ones – in this case those in front should be asked to keep the leader in sight, and told where to wait for further instructions.

It may sometimes be necessary for the leader to ask faster walkers to slow down. Point out that, in the end, the party cannot progress any faster than the pace of its slowest member.

18 The **backmarker** should always remain at the back of the party, if necessary giving encouragement to slower members, and making sure that gates have been closed. The backmarker should notify the leader if any member seems to be having difficulty in keeping up. In an emergency, the backmarker could use a whistle to indicate that the leader should stop – one long blast should be sufficient.

For a change, the leader and backmarker can swap positions during part of the walk.

19 At frequent intervals, and especially at turning points, **look back** to make sure that all the party members are in sight. Try to avoid large gaps occurring, and if necessary slow down the pace. At crucial turning points, or in poor visibility, wait for the backmarker to arrive or come into sight before continuing.

20 Have **rest stops** at suitable points, especially after hill climbs, on reaching roads, after long straight sections or difficult sections. It can be surprising how much a party becomes stretched out at such times, especially if it is a large one, and these stops allow everyone to catch up. They also provide the leader with an opportunity to talk to party members, and for party members to change walking partners.

Do not move off as soon as the backmarker arrives. Wait a few minutes to allow the slower members a rest – they probably have greater need.

21 On re-starting after rest and refreshment stops, **re-count** the number of party members. Keeping track of party members is particularly important in the hills. (See paragraph 4.44 regarding missing members).

22 At intervals **check the time** to see whether you are on schedule. If you are running very late, you may need to take a short cut, especially if you might otherwise miss the opening hours of a pub or tea-room, or your bus or train, or light is fading.

23 When negotiating an **awkward obstruction** such as a dilapidated stile, a wide ditch, or a stream without a bridge, wait to give assistance if required. Members should be

asked to continue a little way ahead to avoid causing embarrassment to the less able-bodied.

24 Make sure that any **dogs** are on a lead when reaching roads or fields containing livestock or in terrain where careful footwork is needed. If necessary, remind the owner that farmers may claim a valid defence if they shoot dogs caught worrying livestock.

25 On reaching **points of interest**, wait for the party to catch up, then briefly impart any knowledge you may have (see paragraphs 2.28 to 2.30). This also provides an opportunity for slower walkers to have a rest, without drawing attention to themselves.

26 In fields **where crops have not been cleared from paths**, providing you are sure of the line of the right of way, ask the party to follow you in single file through the crop. This is preferable to going round the edge of the field, since it reinforces the right of way, and single file minimises crop damage. (See also paragraph 4.15).

Also walk single file over newly tilled ground.

27 When **entering buildings** such as pubs, tea-rooms or buildings of interest, ask the party members to clean, remove or cover muddy boots – some walkers carry plastic bags for this purpose.

28 Before your party members set about getting their refreshments, let them know the **re-start time** and, if necessary, where the meeting point will be. It may be advisable to do this a little way before reaching the lunch

point, as people may otherwise dash off before you have made your announcement.

29 On no account should party members be permitted to eat their **own food** or drink inside a pub, cafe or tea-room, without the permission of the landlord or proprietor – otherwise this gives walkers a bad reputation. On the other hand anyone who wishes to eat their own food should not be made to feel embarrassed, and a suitable place to sit outside should be pointed out.

30 Whether you have a picnic or visit a pub, cafe or tea-room, make sure that you **clear up after your refreshment breaks**. No litter should be left at picnic spots, or anywhere else, by party members.

Pub staff appreciate glasses and plates being taken back to the bar counter. If you need to move tables, always ask permission, and replace them in the original position on leaving. Remember to thank the staff as you leave.

31 If your route passes by or close to **public toilets**, make sure that the party has an opportunity to use them. If you include a pub stop, toilets will be available there.

There are bound to be times of need when no public toilets are available, and advantage will be taken of trees and bushes. This is not normally a problem for men. For women, the leader should discreetly ask the men to continue ahead for a few minutes while the women stop.

32 At some stage during the walk, check that everyone is an **RA member**, especially if there are new faces in the party. Most groups and affiliated clubs have a policy of allowing non-members to join a walk on a trial basis, on the understanding that they will join if they wish to come again. Carry a few copies of the RA recruitment leaflet and your programme to give out if required.

33 Observe reasonable behaviour by following the **Country Code** wherever possible (see box 18, next page). Copies are obtainable from the Countryside Commission, Countryside Council for Wales, or Scottish Natural Heritage (see appendix 5 for addresses).

Box 18

The Country Code

- Enjoy the countryside and respect its life and work
- Guard against all risk of fire
- Fasten all gates
- Keep your dogs under close control
- Keep to public footpaths across farmland
- Use gates and stiles to cross fences hedges, and walls
- Leave livestock, crops and machinery alone
- Take your litter home
- Help to keep all water clean
- Protect wildlife, plants and trees
- Take special care on country roads
- Make no unnecessary noise

Safety considerations

34 Use of **roads** during your walk should be kept to a minimum (see paragraph 2.5). Of course, motorways cannot be used at all by pedestrians.

35 **On reaching a road**, wait for the whole party to catch up, and keep them as close together as possible for all the time you have to use it. If the path or track leads straight into a road with no pavement, wait a little way before the junction so that party members do not rush out into the road.

36 Where crossing a road is unavoidable, especially main ones, always use if available a **protected or controlled crossing**, such as a footbridge, subway, traffic lights or zebra crossing. Remember that a member of the public has no legal power to hold up traffic – only the police or traffic wardens may do this. However, in practice at zebra crossings, it is usually possible to shepherd the whole party across together.

37 If there is **no controlled crossing**, choose a point in the road which provides maximum safety, such as a long straight stretch, the angle of a bend, or the crown of a hill, where the party can be seen by drivers coming from both directions. The leader or backmarker should wait at the crossing point to warn party members of approaching vehicles, and to

make sure that all have crossed safely.

38 If your route continues from one path to another on the far side of a road, close to a bend, station someone at the bend to warn of approaching vehicles.

39 If you have to use a **country road with no pavement or verge**:

i The party should walk in single file, on the right-hand side of the road (as stipulated in the Highway Code). Discourage people from walking two abreast in order to chat.

ii However, there are situations when walking on the right-hand side can be dangerous, especially at right-hand bends, where vehicles driven close to the edge may come into contact with walkers. In such cases the leader should:

- approach the bend with care, moving out a little to check that there is no oncoming traffic
- having passed the bend, signal any oncoming traffic to slow down, using the map at arms length

iii Alternatively, the leader should move carefully to the left-hand side of the road, asking the party to remain on the right. If a vehicle approaches, tell members to wait some distance back from the bend until it has passed. Also warn the vehicle by waving the map up and down.

iv If you have to turn left off the road onto a path shortly after a right-hand bend, it may be practicable for the leader to tell the party to cross to the left-hand side shortly before the bend having first checked that it is safe to do so. During this time the backmarker should watch out for traffic approaching from behind.

v At all times, the party should be warned of the approach of a vehicle: by the leader when from ahead; by the backmarker when from behind. The usual way of doing this is by just shouting "car" – this is effective, whatever kind of vehicle it is. At such times, check that everyone is in single file and keeping well in to the side. Repeat the warnings when vehicles follow in succession.

40 Some paths cross **railway lines** at unguarded crossings. If you have to use one of these:

i Wait until the whole party has caught up before crossing. Explain that they will be using an unguarded railway crossing, and say that it is perfectly legal and safe to do so. Tell everyone to "stop, look and listen" before crossing (there is usually a notice to this effect) and ask them to wait on the far side, beyond the fence.

ii While the party members are crossing, the backmarker should stand away from the near side of the line, and the leader away from the far side, looking out for approaching trains, and making sure that everyone is taking care.

iii Do not continue until you are satisfied that all the party members have crossed safely.

41 **Darkness**: see paragraphs 4.30 to 4.32.

42 **Bad weather**: see paragraphs 4.33 to 4.36.

43 **Do not extend the walk** unless it is convenient for those not wishing to walk further to drop out at the publicised distance.

After the walk

44 On reaching the finish, check that **everyone has been accounted for** and is fixed up with transport.

45 Say that you hope everyone enjoyed the walk, and when the **next one** organised by your group or club will be.

46 If anyone is **not an RA member**, make sure that they have details of how to join (see paragraph 32 above).

47 Hopefully, your party members will now **thank you** for all your time and trouble spent on providing them with an enjoyable day out!

48 Some groups or clubs may ask you to write a **report** on your walk. This will be confirmed by your programme officer if appropriate.

49 If there have been any problems with obstructions or hazards, remind party members to **follow them up** with the appropriate local authority (see paragraph 4.9).

Module 4 : Trouble-shooting

Introduction

1 The inclusion and length of this module should not give a potential leader the idea that leading a walk will be full of problems. In fact **the vast majority of walks are relatively trouble-free** and, if there is a problem, you are likely to find that your party members will accept it with good humour, and do their best to help and co-operate.

Nevertheless, leaders should **be aware** of what could happen, and know what to do if it does. And remember that real emergencies are very rare.

2 If there is a problem, and you have in your party any officers of your RA group or affiliated club, or any other experienced walker, do not be afraid to **consult** them before taking further action.

3 Unless there is some overriding reason for doing otherwise, always **explain** the nature of the problem to your party members, tell them what you propose to do about it, and ask if anyone has any objections.

4 Remember too that, provided they are fully paid up and engaged on RA activities, RA members are *protected* by the **Public Liability Insurance** taken out by the RA in respect of Legal Liability for injury to persons and damage to property of Third Parties caused by negligent acts. The secretary of your RA group or affiliated club, or an RA office (see appendix 5) can provide further details if required.

Note one: It is a condition of the policy that liability for damage or injury should never be admitted.

Note two: The policy provides no cover for personal accidents. Such cover is the responsibility of the individual.

Obstructions and hazards

5 An **obstruction** is anything that prevents walkers from exercising their legal right to pass along a right of way.

Some of these may also be hazardous, by posing the possibility of damage to clothing or injury to walkers.

A **hazard** may not actually prevent you from walking along a path, but may put walkers in danger of injury or damage to clothing etc.

6 Bear in mind that it is **illegal wilfully to obstruct a right of way**, and that bona fide travellers (which include people walking for recreational purposes) are allowed either to remove as much of an obstruction as is necessary in order to pass, or to divert round it.

7 Before taking action to remove, divert round or otherwise avoid an obstruction, you must first **be sure that you are actually on a right of way**. It may have been diverted or closed (see paragraphs 24 to 26 below). You may not be on the exact route of the right of way. If you have no doubt about your exact position on the map, and that you are on a right of way, you should proceed as advised in "Dealing with Obstructions and Hazards" below.

8 Where there is an obstruction, and **you are unsure that you are on a right of way**, this should be clarified by referring to the local authority (see box 14 page 44), your local RA footpath secretary (see the RA Yearbook), or (in Scotland) the Scottish Rights of Way Society (see appendix 5).

9 At the earliest opportunity, **report obstructions** to both the appropriate RA footpath secretary and the appropriate local authority. This will help to get the obstruction cleared – possibly, in minor cases, even in time for the walk you will be leading.

If you find a hazard which is likely to cause serious injury or damage, this should also be reported, even if it is not illegal.

The RA produces a special form 'Reporting Path Problems' – copies can be obtained from an RA office (see appendix 5). Some RA areas and groups, and some local authorities, also have their own path report forms.

Dealing with obstructions and hazards

10 **Barbed wire** may be encountered in several different circumstances:

i Most commonly, it forms the fence on one or both sides of a path. If the path is narrow, and its surface uneven or slippery or both, the wire presents a hazard, although its presence is not illegal unless the path is narrower than the legal width (generally one metre for a footpath, two metres for a bridleway). All you can otherwise do is warn party members to take care.

ii It may be stretched across the line of a right of way – this is illegal. The safest way of dealing with it is to put a coat or piece of rubber over the wire, allowing party members to hold down the wire while they cross over.

One way of getting by!

In fact you would be within your rights to remove enough of the wire to allow passage – just the top strand should be sufficient (with wirecutters if necessary). However, **you must be absolutely certain that you are on the exact route of a right of way, otherwise you lay yourself open to being sued for damage to the landowner's property**.

iii It may be attached along the top bar of a stile, often in a place where it cannot be seen before it is too late, and injury has been caused, or clothing torn. The same advice applies as in (i) and (ii) above, and you should warn party members about the wire.

11 **Blockages** may consist of some major item of refuse, such as an old car, an oil drum or a pile of manure. Deep mud or slurry which spreads over the whole width of a right of way may also be considered a blockage. It may be possible to get round, climb over, or even remove the item, but check whether there are any jagged bits of metal or other protrusion which may cause injury or damage to clothing; or if a barbed wire fence on either side makes it difficult to avoid deep mud. If so, or if the blockage is completely impassable, you should withdraw and find another route rather than risk an injury to a member of your party.

12 **Bulls** of a recognised dairy breed (Ayrshire, British Friesian, British Holstein, Dairy Shorthorn, Guernsey, Jersey and Kerry) are banned from fields crossed by rights of way, except if they are aged less than 10 months. All other breeds and young dairy bulls may be allowed in such fields, but only if accompanied by cows. Of course, you must be sure to recognise the right breed! (See figure 19).

It is probable that the farmer will be abiding by the law, but some members of your party may be terrified by the presence of any bull – if in doubt, or if any bull is on its own, withdraw and find another route.

Do not confuse bulls with **bullocks**, which are young castrated bulls. They usually graze in herds, and may exhibit strong curiosity in you and your party, but are not normally dangerous. If they charge, you should find that if you stand your ground, they will stop a little way short. If you wave your arms up and down, they should run away. If that fails, shout or clap your hands. Bullocks will get more excited if there is a dog in your party – it must be on a lead, and it is advisable to hide it among the party members.

Cows with calves can also be dangerous – never allow your party to pass between a cow and its calf.

13 **Dilapidated or high stiles** can present a problem to the less able-bodied. They are usually surmountable with care,

though you or other party members may need to provide assistance where necessary. Another problem occurs when the landowner puts barbed wire along the top of the stile (see paragraph 10 above). Maintenance of stiles on a right of way is the responsibility of the landowner; if they are not kept in a proper state of repair, the local authority can, after due notice, do the job itself and charge the cost to the landowner.

14 **Electric fences** are sometimes found strung across the middle of a field, in order to keep livestock in a particular part of it. In such cases there should be a strip of rubber over the wire at the point where the right of way crosses. If not, the wire should give no more than a harmless mild shock, and one can often straddle the wire without touching it.

However, some wires run off the mains, and can give a stronger shock, so it is always advisable to lay an article of clothing (or plastic bag or mapcase) over the wire, or use a walking stick, to hold it down for the assurance of less able-bodied party members.

15 **Growing crops**. The farmer has a duty to prevent a crop – other than grass – from making a right of way difficult to find or follow. He must make the line of the path clear and, if crops are growing on it or falling across it, they must be removed. This applies whether it runs through the middle of a field or round the edge. The minimum width required by law if running across the field is: 1 metre for footpaths, 2 metres for bridleways; if at the field edge: 1.5 metres for footpaths, 3 metres for bridleways, though it is rare to find the law correctly complied with.

You have every right to walk through crops growing on a right of way, but you must keep as close as possible to the correct line, in single file. If the path runs across the field, you should not try to go round the field edge, as you will be trespassing, and you are likely to disturb just as much of the crop. Walking through the crop also helps to establish the line of the right of way. If there is a field-edge path or farm track and the right-of-way cross-field path is not re-instated or clear, this constitutes an illegal diversion and should be reported as such (see paragraph 9 above).

Figure 19

This chart is reproduced by permission of *The Countryman*, in which it first appeared.

The Countryman Bull chart

The Ministry of Agriculture's safety division used to warn simply: 'Bulls are always a potential danger, and it is advisable to treat them with extreme caution'.
In 1981 parliament decided that some bulls are 'safe', some not.
But which are which?

DAIRY BREEDS

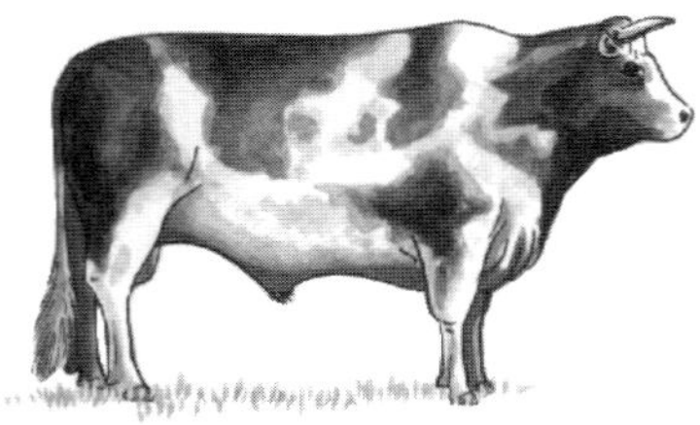

Ayrshire Brown-and-white

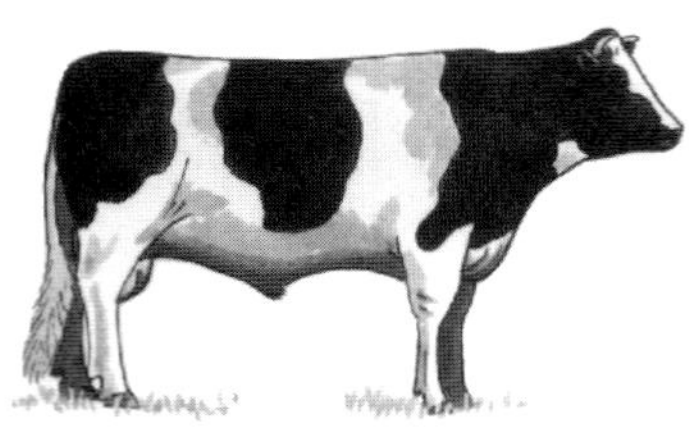

British Holstein Black-and-white

British Friesian Black-and-white

Jersey Pale fawn

Dairy Shorthorn Brown-and-white

Kerry Black

Guernsey Fawn or fawn-and-white

The Wildlife and Countryside Act makes it illegal to have a bull at large in a field containing a public path if it belongs to one of the dairy breeds. But, if the bull is not more than ten months old or if it belongs to a beef breed *and* is with cows or heifers, it is legal.

BEEF BREEDS

Lincoln Red Reddish brown

Hereford Tan with white face

South Devon Brown

Charolais Pale cream

Beef Shorthorn Brown

Aberdeen Angus Black

Welsh Black Black

16 **Intimidation** may be encountered:

i **from a landowner or tenant** who objects to the public walking across his or her land, even when walking on a right of way. It may take the form of verbal or physical threats – though fortunately the latter is rare.

Always remain calm and polite. In most cases, initial aggression on the part of the landowner can be overcome by rational discussion – it may turn out that the path has been legally diverted, and the landowner will gladly tell you where it now runs. But check afterwards with the local authority in case this is an unofficial illegal diversion – see paragraph 8 above.

If intimidation persists, say that you are not aware of any damage being caused. If you believe that you have a legal right to be on the route, either because it is a right of way, or because there is a formal access arrangement, or if there are de facto access traditions (see paragraphs 2.7 to 2.12), say so, and if this is indicated on the map, draw attention to it.

If the landowner says that such rights have been withdrawn legally (see paragraphs 24 to 26 below), this can be checked with the local authority.

If you are sure that your chosen route has a recognised legal or traditional status allowing passage, calmly state that you wish to follow it, unless overriding safety, management or conservation interests can be clearly demonstrated.

If, despite all this, the intimidator persists in unreasonably refusing to let you pass, withdraw and find another route. Do not resort to shouting or abuse. If the landowner threatens violence, it should be reported to the police as well as to the RA footpath secretary and local authority.

ii **from a dog**. Dogs are by nature protective of their territory, though by no means all are fierce or intimidating. Owners are obliged to prevent them from causing damage or injury, and any intimidation is usually in the form of persistent barking from behind a fence, which can be ignored.

If you should find an unleashed and fierce dog in your way, you can either continue confidently (most dogs will back off, especially if there are several people); or carry a stick as a deterrent; or carry an electronic device such as a "Dazer", which emits a high-pitched deterrent whine inaudible to humans. If you have none of these, picking up and pretending to throw a stone or clod of earth can be effective.

17 **Locked gates** are frequently encountered. Check first that the chain fastener cannot be undone (they are often tangled), and that there is no stile nearby (it may be overgrown). If necessary, the party members will have to climb over, one at a time, as near as possible to the hinges, where the gate can take most weight. Be prepared to offer assistance to the less able bodied.

18 **Misleading notices**. You may sometimes see such misleading signs as "Beware of the Bull", "Beware of the Dog", "Private – No Entry" or "Trespassers will be Prosecuted" which have been placed to deter walkers from exercising their rights of access. These could actually apply to adjacent land, but may be erected on a right of way and are therefore illegal. If you are certain that you are on a right of way, you can ignore them. "Private" signs might also include in small lettering "Footpath Only" or words to that effect, implying the presence of a right of way.

In fact, trespassers cannot normally be prosecuted, as trespass is not a criminal offence. Though there are certain exceptions, the most a landowner can do to trespassers (if they are not on a right of way) is to request that they leave the property by the shortest route, and sue them in a civil court if damage has been caused.

19 **Missing signs**. The appropriate local authority has a duty to erect a sign at any point where a right of way joins a metalled road. The type of sign varies widely between authorities, but is usually either a metal or wood "fingerpost", or a low concrete tablet. Unfortunately they are often vandalised, and there have been cases where this has been done by the landowner or farmer to deter walkers. You may find that the fingers have been turned round to point the wrong way (if so, try to turn them back again), or

may be missing, leaving just the post. The low concrete ones may be overgrown – you should try to kick away or beat back the overgrowth.

Some authorities are better than others at erecting these signs. In some areas you may find that none has been erected at any junction.

20 **Missing bridges**. If the stream or ditch can be jumped, you should continue, providing assistance to less abled bodied party members if required. If it is too wide, you may be able to find a narrower part nearby, otherwise you will have to find another route.

21 **Overgrowth**. Paths which are little used tend to become overgrown in summer. Some may be so densely overgrown that they are blocked all year round – in such cases a parallel diversion may have been walked out by regular users. Nettles, brambles and hawthorn are the worst offenders, since they are more likely to cause damage or injury. For minor overgrowth, it is worth carrying a stick or secateurs to beat or cut it back. If the vegetation is too thick to penetrate, you will have to find another route.

RA members clearing a path near Basingstoke

Report the matter to the local authority, who may be able to arrange for the route to be cleared in time for your walk. Many RA areas and groups have regular clearances of overgrowth, and you may find that the local group can organise clearance of the path you wish to use, given sufficient notice.

22 **Ploughed paths**. In autumn and winter, you may well find that paths have been ploughed, and that the furrows make passage awkward, especially if wet. Farmers have a duty to reinstate the line of a right of way within 24 hours (two weeks if the first disturbance for a particular crop). This can easily be done by just running a tractor along the path. If the path has not been reinstated, you should ask the party to walk in single file, as this will beat down the earth or mud and help to establish the line of the path for others.

23 **Use of footpaths by horses, cycles and vehicles** (see paragraph 2.7). On rights of way in England and Wales where horses, cycles and vehicles are excluded, you may find them using the path illegally. Normally this should cause nothing more than annoyance or inconvenience. If damage or injury is caused to any member of your party as a result of such misuse, you should help the person concerned in trying to obtain details so that action can be taken.

On bridleways, keep a look out for horses and cycles (on byways also for vehicles), and if necessary warn your party members to keep clear. Remember that horses have right of way over walkers, and walkers over cyclists.

Remember to report any obstruction, hazard or other deficiency which you may find (see paragraph 9 above).

Diversions and closures

24 If a landowner wishes to divert or close a right of way, a **formal application** must be made to the local authority. If the council agrees to make a legal order to implement the change, a notice must appear in a local paper, and also placed at both ends of the path, allowing at least 28 days for objections. If any objections are received, they must be heard at a public inquiry, or alternatively (if the objectors agree) the matter can be dealt with by written representation.

25 If you find a **diversion or closure notice** on a path, make a note of the details, including the closing date for objections, and the address and telephone number for further information. Pass these on to the local RA footpath secretary (see RA Yearbook), who may not yet be aware of the application, and may wish to register an objection. If any objections have been received, the matter cannot be settled until after a public inquiry or written representations. This could take many months, and it is advisable for you to check on progress with the local authority before finalising your route.

26 If an **application to divert or close a path has been successful**, there is no legal obligation on the landowner or local authority to put up a sign to this effect, though many do so. If there is no sign, you may find that the original route is still passable, and you will be none the wiser unless you are challenged. If you find a sign, or are challenged and told that the right of way has been diverted or closed, you will have to follow the new route of a diverted path, or if it has been closed find a new route.

In any case, if you learn of a closure or diversion, it may be worth making a note of the details (including grid references) and checking with the appropriate local authority whether the diversion or closure is a legal one. Make a note on your map of the closure, or of the new line of a diverted path, and then inform the local RA footpath secretary.

Getting lost

27 **Every leader gets lost** at some time or other, so you should not feel despondent if this happens to you. Never be afraid to admit to your party that you are lost or have taken a wrong turning. Usually they will respond with good humour and sympathy. As long as it does not happen too often!

28 Here is the **recommended procedure** for getting back on the right course:

i Stop, then:

- Try to work out where you are now, by looking more closely at your position.
- Set the map by compass, and get another person to hold it in the set position.
- With the set map, try to identify features that you can see both on map and ground, and use these to work out where you are.
- Use a straight edge (such as the side of your compass) to help in lining up features as seen on ground and map.
- Look for lines of paths on the map that are going in the same direction as the one you are on – one of them might be yours.
- Try to identify some other feature, such as the corner of a wood, a prominent building etc., on both ground and map, then use your straight edge to line up the feature with its symbol on the map – this straight line carries on through your present position on the map.
- Bring into play features that you may hitherto have ignored. Perhaps you did not look at the contours. What are the slopes nearby doing?

ii If all this fails, retrace your steps to the last identifiable point and re-assess your position, possibly re-planning the route from there.

iii In some circumstances, such as in woodland which is not too dense, or in open country, you can make a judgement as to where you are within approximate limits. You may then be able to:

- Follow a compass bearing to an adjoining track or other linear feature.
- Follow the feature to a recognisable point. Though you may be trespassing while following the bearing, you were probably doing so anyway while on the wrong path, and provided you do no damage, this should not matter.

29 Do not be afraid to ask for **advice** from an experienced party member.

Darkness

30 No walk should be planned to finish in darkness. Try to avoid this, if necessary, by shortening the walk. However, this is a real possibility in the event of a delay, particularly outside the period of British Summer Time, and at such times both the leader and backmarker should carry **torches and/or reflective armbands** for use if necessary (see appendix 3).

31 If the **party seems unlikely to reach the finish in daylight**, the leader should ask if any other party members have torches. These people should spread themselves at equal distances along the party, and all torches should be used, either at the approach of a vehicle, to warn it of the party's presence, or to help other party members at dark places where there are difficult surfaces or obstacles.

32 It may be advisable, at the leader's discretion, to **use roads rather than paths** after dusk, as the latter may present more hazards in the dark.

Bad weather

33 It is rare in "moderate conditions" (see Introduction paragraph 10) for bad weather to enforce a change in a leader's plans. However, especially in winter, **listen to weather forecasts** during the few days before your walk, and take appropriate action if necessary:

i If the weather will only affect part of your route, for example a cliff path in high wind, decide on an alternative route.

ii If you are aware of the possibility of severe weather conditions before starting your walk, you should consider the need to abandon it before starting out. If possible, discuss the situation with an officer of your RA group or affiliated club.

iii If possible, try to find an alternative route from the planned meeting point, even if it is much shorter, which can still be undertaken in the prevailing conditions. Then you can still provide people who turn up with a day out.

iv If no alternative is practicable, be prepared to go to the meeting point and apologise to optimistic party members for being unable to provide a walk.

34 If you are caught out by **unexpected bad weather** during your walk, be prepared to change your plans, including shortening the walk, depending on the circumstances.

35 Here is what to do in the most common severe weather circumstances:

i **Thunderstorms**: Avoid hilltops and ridges. Do not shelter under isolated trees or behind prominent rocks, as these tend to be favourite targets of lightning. Otherwise the chances of being struck are very remote, and you should continue your walk as planned.

ii **Blizzards**: Take shelter in a building or woodland until the worst has passed. Check that all your party members are well wrapped up, and if necessary ask if others can lend spare clothing. There is a strong chance of deep snowdrifts on roads, and drivers may not see walkers in such conditions, so try to avoid road walking – you should find that snow is firmer and less deep in open fields. When conditions have eased, take the shortest route, either back to the start for cars, or to the nearest public transport. Be prepared to find cars buried, or public transport out of operation – in this case, contact the police and ask for advice.

iii **Flooding**: After long periods of heavy rain it is quite possible that low-lying land will be flooded, making roads and paths impassable. If the weather is warm and the water not too deep, you may find that your party members are prepared to wade through – they should remove socks, but keep their footwear on in case of sharp stones etc. Otherwise use your map to find usable alternatives around the flooded area.

iv **Swollen streams**: This factor may affect your choice of route in upland areas where many paths cross small streams by stones on the stream bed rather than a bridge. In a period of high rainfall there is often the risk that streams will rise to make such crossings at least uncomfortable and maybe impossible. Streams rise during heavy rain remarkably quickly and subside again somewhat more slowly afterwards.

36 If in doubt, **contact the local police** for advice about road conditions in the area you plan to visit, and the local RA secretary about the state of the paths.

Travel problems

37 If you are using public transport, it is possible that the bus or train you are aiming for could be **cancelled**. If the service is reasonably frequent, there should not be too much hardship in waiting for the next service.

38 If there is a delay of several hours, or there are no more buses or trains that day, you may need to arrange an **alternative means** of transport, though any extra costs involved would be the responsibility of individual party members.

39 The first thing to do is **contact the bus or train operator** (get the telephone number from Directory Enquiries). If a service has been cancelled, resulting in hardship, they may in the interests of goodwill be willing to provide a suitable private vehicle to transport your party to a point where onward transport is available. If any party member still has difficulty getting home, be prepared to offer advice – though it is their own responsibility to take matters further with the transport operator, making a claim for expenses incurred if necessary.

40 If necessary, be prepared to arrange **private hire transport** yourself:

i If you have access to a Yellow Pages or Thomson Directory, this will provide details of taxi, minibus and coach operators in your area. Otherwise you can call "Talking Pages", a 24-hour nationwide service operated by Yellow Pages (Phone 0345-600900). Get the telephone numbers of two or three suitable operators in your area.

ii Call the operators to see which can send help most quickly, and ask for an estimate of the cost. Discuss the situation with your party, making it clear that each member will have to contribute their share.

41 If the lack of transport is the **fault of the bus or train operator**, it may be possible to obtain a refund on behalf of the party members.

i Make it clear that you are doing this as a courtesy, and that no guarantee can be given.

ii Get a receipt for the charges incurred.

iii Take the names and addresses of your party members.

iv Write a polite letter to the operator explaining the circumstances. Say that you feel that reimbursement should be made of necessary expenses incurred. Enclose the receipt and list of names and addresses, and ask for the reimbursement to be sent direct to each party member.

42 If the **bus or train operator is not at fault**, no reimbursement will be due. Apologise to the party, even if you also are not at fault. If anyone feels aggrieved and asks for compensation, it will have to be pointed out that (as should be stated in any programme or publicity) they will have come at their own risk.

The circumstances should be reported to the group or club committee. If they consider it appropriate and within reason, they may think it worthwhile for the sake of goodwill to pay some compensation from group or club funds.

Party members

43 If anyone at the meeting point is obviously grossly **ill-prepared or ill-suited** for the conditions:

i Start by asking them discreetly if they have done anything of this kind before, and, if so, how they got on.

ii If necessary, strongly but politely advise them not to come – leaders have the full support of the RA in this. Try to suggest something else to do in the area, which may be more suitable.

iii If such a person insists on coming, say that they do so at their own risk, and that you cannot accept any responsibility for the consequences. Remember that you cannot actually forbid anyone to walk with you.

44 If a **party member goes missing,** discovered perhaps as a result of a periodic check (see paragraph 3.21):

i Get the group to stop.

ii Call out or whistle, in case the missing person is nearby but out of sight.

iii Send a couple of people back, perhaps including the backmarker, asking them to return within fifteen minutes if they do not find the missing person.

iv If the missing person is not found, the party should continue, either still under the control of the leader, or of the backmarker, or of some other person who knows the route. Arrangements for getting in contact again at the end of the walk should be made.

v The search party should then go back along the route as far as necessary.

vi If the missing person is not found, depending on the circumstances and any knowledge of the missing person:

- It may be advisable to contact the police at the earliest opportunity, using your judgement and bearing in mind the weather, terrain and location.
- If you feel confident that the person is capable of finding

their own way to the finishing point, or of getting home by some other means, try to make contact at the finish or on returning home, and then if this fails contact the police.

- It should be noted that the police may not be able to take immediate action unless they feel that the missing person is in a vulnerable situation, e.g. very young, elderly, incapable of getting home without help, or in adverse weather conditions.
- The police will require as detailed a description as possible of the missing person, i.e. as much as you know including name, age, home address, what the person was wearing, the place where last seen, and under what circumstances the person went missing.

Note: This is when the list of names (see paragraph 3.16) comes in useful.

45 Party members who are tired, or need to get home early, may wish to **take a different route** from the one you have planned. If you feel that, by doing so, they may put themselves at risk of getting lost, or of getting into a dangerous situation, you should try to discourage them. Otherwise:

i Make sure that they have a map, or detailed route instructions (write them down if necessary).

ii If necessary, ask your backmarker or another experienced party member with a map to accompany them.

iii If you are not satisfied that the member is doing the right thing, try to dissuade, but remember that you cannot forbid anyone from leaving.

iv Do everything possible to ensure that any route they may take does not lead into danger.

v If any members insist on going their own way against your advice, say that they do so at their own risk.

vi If there is a general desire to follow a different route, or take a short cut, listen to the argument of the "breakaway faction", then make a decision and give your reasons for it. If necessary, follow the procedure given in (i) to (v) above.

46 If a party member **causes offence** to others, politely ask him or her to desist, as such behaviour is spoiling the enjoyment of the others. If your first action fails, on reaching a point where it is possible for the member to take transport, you could try saying that the person's presence is not welcome and suggest that they leave – hopefully they will act accordingly.

47 Bear in mind that **odd behaviour** may indicate some form of illness or distress, perhaps due to exposure if the person is inadequately dressed in cold weather, or to inability to cope with a problem. If you suspect this to be the case, speak to the person discreetly, and try to find out if there is any way you can help.

48 If necessary, **seek the advice and support** of a group or club officer, or other experienced party member.

Accidents and injuries

49 It is in everyone's interest for as many walkers as possible to be qualified in **first aid**. The RA encourages its groups and affiliated clubs to arrange for any interested member to undertake a first aid course organised by St. John Ambulance or British Red Cross – both are willing to organise special courses for RA areas and groups.

50 Groups and clubs should also encourage their members to carry a small **first aid kit** for self-treatment of minor injuries. The minimum contents of a first aid kit should be:

- three sterile unmedicated ambulance dressings of different sizes
- two triangular bandages and safety pins
- strips of elastoplast of various widths
- individually wrapped antiseptic moist cleaning wipes
- small scissors

51 In the event of an accident, whether serious or not, **establish whether any party member is a qualified first aider**.

52 **Minor cuts and blisters** can be treated from a standard first aid or blister kit, after cleaning as well as possible. The injured person should be advised, on returning home, to

clean, disinfect and cover the wound again, also, especially if the cut is deep, to seek medical advice – the need for an anti-tetanus injection must always be considered. If the injury appears to be causing distress, the leader should arrange for the person to obtain qualified help as soon as possible.

53 With **more serious injuries**, or an incident such as a heart attack or epileptic fit, or if the casualty is unconscious:

i The first thing to do is to check that he or she is breathing, and that the airway is kept clear, removing any obstruction if necessary.

ii Call for an ambulance, if necessary from a private house with a telephone. Send at least two other party members to do this, writing down for them the following information:

- a description of your location (including grid reference)
- time of incident
- the suspected nature of the injury
- the sex, approximate age and (if possible) name of the casualty
- the number of people left with the casualty

If these people need to go some distance, make sure that they have a map and can read it.

iii The leader (and if appropriate another party member who is qualified in first aid) should stay with the casualty. Ask your backmarker, or another experienced walker, to take over as leader, so that the rest of the party can continue their walk or return home as preferred.

iv The new leader should immediately take the rest of the party 100 metres or so away, so that the situation can be discussed out of earshot. A situation in which everyone is trying to offer advice should be kindly but firmly avoided. Of course, relatives and close friends of the casualty should be allowed to stay.

v If someone is trained to do so, the casualty can be put in a recovery position. Avoid the temptation to get him or her to sit up or get to their feet, unless you are absolutely certain that it is safe. In this case, a reassuring posture is to let the casualty sit, leaning onto an able-bodied party member.

vi Do not move the casualty unless he or she is in a dangerous position. Keep him or her as warm and comfortable as possible, using spare clothing lent by other party members if necessary, paying attention to a waterproof and warm layer under the casualty. Give reassurance that help is on its way. If you or any party member has a lightweight foil blanket or bivvy bag, use it.

54 If a party member with a minor sickness or injury **wishes to return home** as soon as possible, and can still walk, follow the advice contained in paragraph 45 above, but make sure that the person is accompanied.

55 If an accident takes place in a situation where you cannot go or send someone for help, you should **use your whistle** (or torch at night) to attract attention. The approved procedure in emergencies is to give six blasts or flashes in quick succession, repeated every minute. The approved response, meaning "message understood", is three blasts or flashes in quick succession, repeated every minute.

This procedure is normally used in mountains. Whilst it may not be understood by people living nearby in "moderate conditions", it is better to use it than do nothing – the chances are that someone will realise that help is needed.

MODULE 5 : WALKS FOR THE PUBLIC

Introduction

1 From time to time, experienced leaders may be asked to organise and lead, on behalf of the Ramblers' Association, a walk which **members of the public** will be invited to join. Some areas and groups organise such walks regularly, as they provide an ideal opportunity to introduce non-members to the activities of the RA.

2 These walks may be part of an RA nationwide event, such as **Family Rambling Day** (usually the last Sunday in June, to encourage families to take up walking) or **Forbidden Britain Day** (usually the last Sunday of September, to draw attention to paths and areas where access is obstructed, unreasonably prevented or in danger of being lost); or the **National Trust and RA Christmas Walks**. Or they may have some special local purpose, such as the official opening of a new walking route.

Family Rambling Day near Portsmouth

3 It must be stressed that only **experienced leaders** should lead such walks, as they will be better able to cope with any difficulties that may arise.

4 **All that has been learned in Modules 2, 3 and 4 applies**. Yet, however experienced a leader may be, when members of the public are invited, there is more to be considered in

connection with the walk, as described in this module.

5 As it is often difficult to predict how many people will attend such walks, it is sensible to **keep the route as simple as possible**, to minimise the difficulties in managing a large number of people.

6 If a large attendance is expected, it is highly advisable to **discuss the route with the local police**, especially if much walking on or near public roads is necessary, or parking for a large number of cars has to be arranged. They may advise that the organisers should provide sufficient stewards to be spread at intervals along the party.

Before the walk

7 The prime responsibility for promoting a public walk usually lies with the area or group **publicity officer**. However, the leader will need to provide information, and may be asked to help prepare the material. The following paragraphs will be useful.

8 A **reconnaissance** is essential for any walk for members of the public (see paragraphs 2.50 to 2.54). The leader should then bear in mind if necessary any special factors, such as those mentioned in paragraph 10 below.

9 The leader will need to supply all the **information mentioned in paragraph 2.60** for inclusion in any material produced for the event, such as leaflets, posters and press releases. These should also mention the reason for the walk, and state that no charge is made by the RA for going on it.

10 Further information may be needed about the **suitability** of the walk for families with children or people with disabilities, including (if appropriate) whether the route is negotiable by pushchairs or wheelchairs; also whether dogs can be taken.

11 If the walk includes a **planned stop** in order to visit a place of interest, or for a celebrity speech, this should be mentioned in the advance publicity material.

12 If a **place of interest** is to be visited, the leader will need to provide a brief description, details of any admission fees for adults and children, and if appropriate whether it is accessible to pushchairs and wheelchairs. Say if the place is run by the National Trust or similar organisation so that members know to bring their membership cards. If a large number is expected it is advisable to check with the establishment that the party can be accommodated.

13 The publicity for some **RA national events** such as Family Rambling Day or Forbidden Britain Day will be organised centrally by the RA. However, much can still be done at local level to increase the attendance, such as putting leaflets or posters in libraries, sending press releases to local media. Much advice is contained in a Publicity Pack available from the RA's London office – the area or group publicity officer may already have a copy of this.

14 If necessary, be prepared to help the publicity officer make up a **special leaflet.** This may apply if supplies of suitable literature cannot be obtained in time for your walk, or if existing material does not suit your purpose. If you have any suitable photos available, include them in your leaflet. The Publicity Pack (see paragraph 13) provides guidance on preparing and printing such leaflets, and the cost will be borne by your area or group. In some cases a grant may be available from an RA office (see appendix 5).

The Publicity Pack also includes a blank poster, which can be used to carry the special leaflet. Bulk supplies are available from the London office. If this is unsuitable, or cannot be obtained in time, make sure that your leaflet at least includes the RA logo, which can be cut from a letterhead or another leaflet (sheets of logos are also available from the London office).

15 Any publicity material should include a **disclaimer**, e.g. "Members of the public attend the walk at their own risk". Whilst this is unlikely to be an effective protection against legal action in the event of injury or damage, it does serve to remind people of the possibility of such accidents, and that they should take care. (See also paragraph 4.4 concerning **public liability insurance**).

16 Make sure that you have a supply of suitable **RA literature** to hand out to non-members on the day, especially the RA recruitment leaflet, which describes the aims and activities of the RA, as well as the benefits of membership, and also includes a membership application form. Supplies of this and other literature can be obtained from your area or group publicity officer, or from the RA's offices.

The day of the walk

17 All the points mentioned in **Module 3** apply, with the following additions.

18 Be sure to **arrive early** at the meeting point. Some people who are new to walking are likely to get there early, and may need assurance that they are in the right place. You can also use this time to hand out literature about the RA.

19 When you **thank everyone for attending**, at the meeting point or at a suitable quiet point shortly after setting off, be sure to mention that the walk has been organised by the Ramblers' Association. If the walk is for a special purpose (such as Family Rambling Day or Forbidden Britain Day), briefly outline its purpose and promise some literature at the end.

20 Ask if any **representatives of the press** are present. They will probably introduce themselves to you anyway. Make a note of their names, whom they represent, and a telephone number. Ask if they need any special photo stops. Be prepared to help them as much as possible, but do not let them hold up the party too long.

21 The walk provides an ideal opportunity for **promoting the Ramblers' Association**. This can be done by:

i Handing out appropriate RA literature (see paragraph 16 above) at a planned rest or refreshment stop, and again at the finish.

ii Giving a short talk about the RA, and if appropriate the purpose of the day's event. This could be done by a committee member if present.

iii Talking casually to individual non-members during the walk about the benefits of RA membership. For this purpose it is a good idea for as many committee members as possible to attend, to give support to the leader and backmarker.

22 Be prepared for enthusiastic potential members who wish to **join on the spot**. Help them fill in the membership application form in the RA recruitment leaflet (see paragraph 16 above), and either tell them to send it to the RA's London office, or, if you think it will "clinch the sale", take it yourself to send on, together with the appropriate subscription, giving a written receipt.

23 Make a note of anything which may be suitable for a **press release** after the event, such as any celebrities who attended (ask their permission for being mentioned), or any unusual (but not unfavourable) occurrences.

24 **Photographs** may also be needed, both in connection with the press release, and for other publicity activities. If you do not take any yourself, see if anyone else in your party is doing so. Ask if they would be willing to lend any suitable photos, and take their name and telephone number to pass on to the publicity officer.

After the walk

25 Let your publicity officer have some information about your walk so that it can be used in a **press release**. This may include the number of people who attended, how many of these were children, and any other points of interest (see paragraphs 23 to 24 above).

26 If any press representatives attended the walk, try to get hold of any resulting articles, and pass them on to your area or group publicity officer.

27 In the unlikely event of an **incident of a controversial nature**, contact the Press Officer of the appropriate RA office (see appendix 5) as soon as possible for advice.

SECTION C : TRAINING

Module 6: Organising and running a course

Introduction

1 Many areas and groups of the Ramblers' Association already organise informal courses on navigation and leadership. We hope that many more of them, as well as affiliated clubs and other organisations wishing to expand their activities into walking, will decide to do the same, using this manual as a guide.

Advice is given on the types of course, the costs involved, finding an organiser or tutor, class size, duration, equipment, teaching techniques, practical exercises and publicity.

2 It is intended that such courses will concentrate on the **basic techniques** involved in both navigation and leadership, thereby enabling participants to take their first steps in map reading, or in organising and leading a walk for their group or club.

3 **Courses based on this manual** would normally take place over several weeks, with weekly evening sessions interspersed with practical daytime ones. They are intended to complement, and not compete with, those organised by other organisations, as listed in appendix 2. For some course members, such a course will be sufficient for their needs.

4 Other course members, having learned from this manual the basic facts and techniques, may wish to expand their knowledge and improve their techniques by participating in one of the **award schemes or courses** listed in appendix 2, and perhaps obtain thereby an award or certificate.

Establishments offering residential courses can put participants through intensive training over a relatively short period, in surroundings which are ideally suited, both for indoor and outdoor exercises, and for the attractiveness of the countryside.

Help from the RA panel

5 The RA has an experienced **Advisory Panel** on Navigation and Leadership. Its members are willing to advise RA areas, groups and affiliated clubs which are contemplating the organisation of courses on these subjects. There are two stages when such help and advice would be most appropriate:

i At the outset of the initiative.

ii Immediately before the finalisation of preparations for the course.

Further details can be obtained from the RA's London office (see appendix 5).

Types of course

6 This manual can be used as a basis for organising two types of course: informal and formal.

7 **Informal** courses are those organised by an RA area or group, affiliated club or other organisation purely for the benefit of its members. They may be held over a series of evenings at the home of the organiser, or one of the participants, or in a hired room; or during a weekend using a youth hostel or other establishment providing accommodation. Certain items of teaching equipment (see paragraph 31 below) would have to be provided by the organisers.

8 **Formal** courses are organised as evening classes in conjunction with a college of further education, or an adult education authority or similar body, using their premises; and probably their teaching equipment (paragraph 31 below). Such courses would be available to members of the public, and the usual charges would apply.

Note: Colleges of further education are now "incorporated". This makes them independent of local authorities, and may affect their ability or willingness to provide subsidised courses of this type.

Formal courses might include only the navigation modules of this manual, as leadership could be considered too specialised a subject by education authorities, who require a broad market for their courses.

9 Whether formal or informal, all courses must include a number of daytime practical sessions.

Costs

10 The costs and expenses of organising an **informal** course would either have to be borne by the organisers, or shared between the participants. These may have to cover, as required:

i Hire of a room.

ii Hire of teaching equipment.*

iii One-off costs of setting up the course, e.g. provision of maps, slides etc. *

iv Duplication of handouts.*

* See paragraph 31 below.

For courses organised by RA areas and groups (but not affiliated clubs or other organisations) for the benefit of members only, the RA can often give financial support – contact an RA office (see appendix 5) or your local RA area or group secretary for details.

11 The costs of a **formal** course would be borne by the education authority. The lecturer would receive the authority's usual fee for his or her services, but would be expected to bear the one-off costs of setting up the course (see paragraph 10 iii above).

On a formal course, students may be expected to bear the costs themselves of handouts (see paragraph 31 vii below), the map on which the instruction is based, and of travelling to the outdoor practicals.

12 Whichever type of course is involved, any adaptation of a published book or map for teaching purposes, including photocopying, will require permission from the publishers,

and probably incur the payment of **royalties**.

This particularly concerns Ordnance Survey maps if they are to be photocopied or adapted, but not of course their normal use in map reading exercises. The OS are happy for one photocopy to be taken for teaching purposes, but more than this will require special permission, and may involve a royalty charge. For further details contact the Copyright Branch of the Ordnance Survey in Southampton (telephone 0703-792028).

It may be worth obtaining an example of the local authority's definitive map (see box 14, page 44) for teaching purposes.

13 It is worth seeking to defray the costs of running a course through **sponsorship** by, for example, equipment manufacturers, or local businesses such as outdoor equipment shops, which may benefit from their association with the course.

Finding an organiser and/or tutor

14 Naturally, any RA area, group or affiliated club wishing to organise and run a course must find **someone who is willing to take on the commitment**, possibly without remuneration, of setting up and teaching the course. It may be possible to divide these functions between two or more people.

15 The **tutor** must be an experienced navigator and leader. A member of your group or club may be able and willing. Other sources may include neighbouring groups or clubs, your area committee, colleges of further education, or outdoor activity centres.

Size of classes

16 There is no reason why an experienced leader should not use this manual as the basis for introducing a "class" of just **one or two friends** to the arts of map reading and leadership, though the use of equipment will be constrained by availability and cost.

17 For **informal courses** run by RA areas, groups and affiliated clubs, in order to make a course worthwhile from the points of view of effort and cost, it is necessary to take as many participants as is reasonable, without prejudicing the ability of the tutor to give due attention to the individual needs of participants on practical exercises.

Three or four course members would provide an ideal tutor-student ratio, and we suggest that there should not be more than twelve. Much will depend on the capacity of the premises to be used as a classroom, and the tutor's experience and preference.

18 For **formal courses** run by an education authority, the number will depend on the authority's policy regarding the minimum number to make a class viable. In some cases this may be as high as fourteen. The authority should be persuaded not to take on more than 20 course members, and in this case assistant tutors would be needed.

19 It may be possible to **increase the number of participants** if two or more tutors are available, especially for the practical exercises. In larger classes the quicker and more experienced course members may be able to help the others – this also encourages a mutually supportive atmosphere.

Duration and content

20 A **map-reading course** can be spread over several weeks in the form of a number of evening sessions plus some outdoor practicals. A suggested programme for an extended course (consisting of 5 x 2-hour evening sessions plus 2 x 1-day practical sessions) appears in box 20. This can be extended if required to cover various aspects of leadership.

21 A **leadership course** could similarly be spread over several weeks, if required, with 2 or 3 x 2-hour evening sessions plus one full day outdoor session. Alternatively (and perhaps more satisfactorily) it could take the form of an intensive weekend course. This could take place in the home locality of the participants, but can be more effective (though more expensive) if run residentially at a suitable centre, such as a youth hostel or field study centre, thus providing a pleasant

and stimulating atmosphere more conducive to learning.

Leadership training is best carried out through discussions and practical exercises. A suggested programme appears in box 21. Course publicity should state that intending participants must already be reasonably accomplished at map reading.

22 It may be worth considering a **1-day introductory course** as an appetiser, so that people interested can get an idea whether to proceed to a lengthier commitment later on. This could be spent partly indoors on theory, but should include a significant practical at the end.

The introductory course could be followed up by one or more outdoor events in the group or club programme, specially for map reading practice and leadership techniques. In the meantime, participants should be invited to study this manual at home.

23 You may wish to **adapt these methods** to suit your requirements, or those of the education authority, but all the aspects of navigation and leadership covered by sections 1 and 2 of this manual are candidates for inclusion.

24 The modular nature of the manual makes it possible to **omit subjects** in which course members already have some expertise. For example, experienced map-readers may wish to learn only route planning or leadership techniques; or course members not wishing to lead can study just the modules covering navigation.

Box 20

Suggested map reading course syllabus

References to paragraphs in modules of this manual take the same form used in the body of the text, e.g. "2.14" for module 2 paragraph 14. Letters prefixing the reference are: "I" for introduction; "A" for appendix; and "PE" for practical exercise. In this case a reference of e.g. "PE 1.4" means module 1 practical exercise 4.

Week 1 *(indoors)*

Introduction . Aims of the course . Types of countryside covered (I 10). Equipment needed (A3). What is a map? (1.2). Types of map for walkers (1.4 to 1.7). Scales (1.3). Grid references (1.22 to 1.31). Points of the compass. Map symbols (1.12, 2.7 to 2.12).

Practical exercises: reading a map (PE 1.1); verbalising a route (PE 1.4).

Week 2 *(indoors)*

Contours (1.15 to 1.21). Setting a map (1.43). Navigation drill (PE 1.7). Introduction to compasses (map to ground) (1.32 to 1.36). Slide show (6.38).

Practical exercise: contours (PE 6.12).

Week 2 *(outdoors)*

Morning (as a class): navigation practice; taking turns to lead; relating map to countryside; taking compass bearings (PE 6.13).

Afternoon (individual): simple orienteering exercise (PE 6.14)

Week 3 *(indoors)*

Review of compass use (1.32 to 1.36). Magnetic variation (Box 8). Checking path direction (1.36). Walking on a bearing (Box 6). More contour practice (1.15 to 1.21). What makes a good route (2.5 to 2.6). Setting objectives (2.45). Recognising good walking areas (figures 15 and 16). Measuring distances on the map (1.44). Log book. Estimating walking time (2.19 to 2.22). How to obtain maps (1.4 to 1.10).

Week 4 *(indoors)*

Lunch stop (2.37 – 2.43). Recording the route (2.55). Rights of way (2.7 to 2.10). Obstructions and hazards (4.5 to 4.23). Path reports (4.9). The Ramblers' Association. Slide show (6.38).

Practical exercise: planning a route (PE 2.9, PE 2.10).

Week 4 *(outdoors)*

Morning (in pairs or singly): navigate set routes with quiz.

Afternoon (in pairs or singly): walk own planned route.

Week 5 *(indoors)*

Debrief on Week 4 *outdoors*. Measuring distances on the ground (1.44viii). If lost? (4.27 to 4.29). Slide show (6.38). Hill navigation.

Box 21

Suggested leadership course syllabus

Discussion topics

1 Why do you wish to lead?

2 What does a leader do? (section B)

3 Route selection (module 2)

4 What information should a leader acquire?

- legal rights (2.7 to 2.13, 4.4)
- what is happening in the countryside?
- some background to the RA

5 What are the general leadership skills? (module 3)

- communicating from leader to party members and vice versa
- making decisions
- keeping the party together
- where should the leader be?
- walking on and crossing roads

Course Members should be encouraged to work out their own ideas, with the tutor correcting and providing additional information when appropriate.

6 Functions of a backmarker (2.54, 3.18)

Practical exercises

1 *Indoors*. Each course member gives a short briefing on a ramble of their own devising, pointing out the route and matters of interest, and answering questions from the rest of the group. Time allowed: 10 minutes per course member.

2 *Indoors*. Each course member gives a short talk as if at the meeting point (see paragraph 3.5). Time allowed: 5 minutes per course member.

3 *Outdoors*. Course members take it in turns to be leader and backmarker. They consider and discuss their responsibilities. At the same time the person appointed leader will be navigating and the rest of the party following the route on their own maps. Time allowed: 30 minutes per course member.

4 *Outdoors*. Simulate an injury or a missing person. There need be no warning given. Every step taken should be discussed and there should be a full discussion at the end. Point out how time flies in such situations. Time allowed: 1.5 hours.

Publicity for your course

25 Give your course a **snappy but accurate title** e.g. "Map & Compass for Walkers" or "Navigation & Leadership for Ramblers". Also provide a brief synopsis in two or three sentences for inclusion in publicity material.

26 Publicity for an **informal course** is mainly a matter for the committee of the area, group or club concerned. Usually details will appear in its programme or newsletter, and perhaps also in that of the area or region, if members of other groups are to be invited.

27 If yours is a **formal course**, organised in conjunction with an education authority, they will handle all the publicity arrangements. However you will be asked to supply a brief synopsis of your course for the prospectus. Look at last year's prospectus to get an idea of the "house style" – this should enable you to maximise the impact of your synopsis within its constraints. Make sure to specify any map that students should bring to the first session.

Ensure that publicity produced by an education authority makes clear that the course is "organised in conjunction with the Ramblers' Association".

28 The organiser and tutor can help to promote the course by:

i Making announcements during group or club walks and social events.

ii Preparing a small duplicated leaflet to hand out to anyone who may be interested: make sure that it includes details of what subjects are to be covered, dates, times, location and any charges, as well as items of equipment that participants will need to bring. Include a contact address or telephone number and say that those interested should contact you by a certain cut-off date (at which time you will need to decide whether there is enough interest to proceed).

iii Providing details to your RA regional, area or group newsletter.

29 There is also an opportunity to **promote membership of the RA** by:

i Sending a press release about your course to local newspapers and radio. This must be done in consultation with your area or group committee, which may have an officer responsible for publicity; and also if appropriate with the education authority. Make sure that the press release includes the same details as mentioned in paragraph 28 (ii).

If the course is an informal one for members only, stress that anyone interested must join the RA to participate – the other benefits of RA membership can then be mentioned too. Include a contact name and telephone number for further information.

ii On any course which may be attended by non-members:

- taking copies of appropriate RA literature, especially the RA recruitment leaflet (see paragraph 5.16);
- using a montage of photographs of obstructions and clearance work to illustrate the problems being tackled by the RA.

Equipment needed

30 For any course involving map reading, it is necessary to get hold of certain items of equipment. Some are used by the tutor only; others must be provided by each participant.

31 The **tutor** will need to provide:

i An overhead projector and screen.*

ii Foils or acetate sheets for use with (i).*

iii Maps: examples of Pathfinder, Landranger, Outdoor Leisure and possibly Harveys. Also (at tutor's discretion) examples of orienteering maps.

iv Map sections for practical work – they could be either cut-outs or photographs.•

v Compasses: examples – this could be just one suitable compass, but preferably various types if available.

vi Photographs of path obstructions and other leadership problems (opportunities for humour here).

vii Duplicated hand-outs, e.g. syllabus, course notes, equipment notes, map notes, grid reference notes etc., complying with any copyright conditions.

* For formal courses, the education authority may be able to provide these items.

- Map extracts for slides or prints can easily be photographed by mounting the camera on an enlarger stand and fitting a close-up lens. The Ordnance Survey would not normally charge a copyright fee for this, but they ask to be informed (see paragraph 12 above).

32 **Participants** will each need to have or obtain:

i One or more suitable maps as required.*

ii Map-case.*

iii Suitable compass.*

iv Basic walking gear for practical sessions, i.e. footwear, rucksack and appropriate clothing.*

v Notebook, pen, pencil, ruler, eraser.

vi Magnifying glass (optional).

* The tutor will give advice on these items during the first session.

Teaching techniques

33 The way in which any subject is absorbed by the course members depends very much on the way it is taught – in such a way as to make it stick in the mind. Individual tutors may well have their own ideas about this, but we give here some suggestions as a guide.

34 **Encourage a mutually supportive and co-operative atmosphere**, both between the tutor and course members, and between course members themselves.

35 **Humour** and a light touch can play an important role in effective teaching, and we hope that the cartoons in this manual will help in this respect. Keep an eye out during your own walks and everyday lives for anything that can be turned into a humourous aid to your teaching. Build up a stock of standard (to you!) jokes to be wheeled out at the appropriate moments.

36 **Local practice.** Set practical exercises using the Pathfinder map for the course members' home locality (some suggestions are included in this manual).

37 **Homework** using theoretical local leadership situations. For example:

i Find out train and bus times for a day trip to a specified destination (British Rail, county council bus enquiry line).

ii Find out which local contractors have taxis and minibuses for hire (Yellow Pages, Thomson Directory, tourist information centre).

iii List official car-parking opportunities in a specified area (shown on maps; tourist information centre).

iv To whom would one report an obstruction on a particular path? (which RA group, local authority).

v List pubs and tea-rooms in a specified locality, together with their telephone numbers (Yellow Pages, Thomson Directory, tourist information centre).

vi Obtain some free literature about places of interest in a specified area (regional tourist board, tourist information centre).

38 **Demonstrating a walk by slides**

i On a walk, the tutor takes photographs at a number of sensible points, e.g. the way ahead, view to the right, entering a farmyard etc.

ii At home, a series of slides is prepared, photographing the relevant map extract for each slide with the map appropriately orientated (see footnote • to paragraph 31 above).

iii In class, two projectors and two screens permit simultaneous viewing of each pair. The tutor points out what is to be seen from the map and how it relates to the countryside. Students can also be asked questions.

Practical exercises

The following practical exercises are suitable only for class use. See also those following modules 1 and 2.

Practical exercise 12:

Contour quiz

Indoors. The tutor devizes a quiz, on an A4 sheet of paper, depicting a set of landforms by means of contours. Questions such as "Can you see Point A from Point B?", or "Is the form X to Y a spur or a valley?", or "Describe the rise and fall of the path from G to H". These test the course members' contour interpretation skills and provide practice.

Time allowed: 30 minutes.

Practical exercise 13:

Group outing

Outdoors. This is a suitable first practical in which the class walks a route together, ideally in an area having many well marked paths. There should be frequent points where route-finding decisions are needed. Each class member has his or her own copy of the relevant map and knows the route to be taken. Both Landranger and Pathfinder maps could be used to familiarise course members with both types. Each class member takes it in turn to lead a leg of the route, using "Routefinding Drill" (see practical exercise 1.7), while another acts as backmarker. At times the class pauses to practise: setting the map; relating map to country; look at contours on the map and relate them to land-shape; examine any discrepancies between map and ground; taking first compass bearings.

Time allowed: 2.5 hours.

Practical exercise 14:

Basic orienteering

Outdoors. Course members take bearings from the map, and check them against the path direction on the ground, in an area having a dense network of paths marked on a Pathfinder map (common land may be suitable). The tutor places beforehand notices bearing letters of the alphabet on trees at path junctions. The course members individually visit each junction in any order, using the compass for direction-finding on each leg, noting the letters.

Classroom instruction on taking a bearing from the map is repeated immediately before the course members set off. Magnetic variation can be ignored.

Time allowed: 1.5 hours.

Practical exercise 15: **Complex orienteering**

Outdoors. As for practical exercise 14, but going off-path at times. A more difficult terrain should be chosen, so that good contour interpretation and compass work can be emphasised. This exercise is suitable for advanced students, and requires a high standard of course setting from the tutor.

Time allowed: 1.5 hours.

Practical exercise 16: **Route briefing**

Each course member briefs the class on his or her planned route, using practical exercise 9 in module 2 as a basis, then answers questions.

Time allowed: 10 minutes per person.

Practical exercise 17: **At the meeting point**

Course Members talk to the class about their planned routes, as if they were at the meeting point (paragraph 3.5iii).

Time allowed: 5 minutes per person.

Practical exercise 18: **Injury or missing person simulation**

Simulate an injury, or a missing person situation – no warning need be given. Every step taken should be discussed, and there should be a full discussion afterwards. Point out how time flies in such situations.

Time allowed: 1.5 hours.

APPENDIX 1 : FURTHER READING

Titles are shown in bold text, followed in brackets by: the author (where appropriate); publisher, with telephone number for further information. The full address of many of these organisations is shown in the address directory in the RA Yearbook. A brief summary of the contents is given. All details are correct at time of going to press.

Items marked * are not available in bookshops, and must be ordered direct from the publisher

GENERAL

Instant Weather Forecasting (Alan Watts; Harper Collins 081-741 7070). A clear and concise guide to weather patterns and forecasting changes.

Out in the Country* (Countryside Commission Publications 0604-781848). Free pocket guide to rights of way and countryside access matters.

Rambler's Yearbook & Accommodation Guide (Ramblers' Association 071-582 6878). Annual guidebook, free to members, also on public sale. Includes details of: RA organisation; area and group secretaries; legal rights in the countryside; long distance paths; public transport; Ordnance Survey maps; equipment shops; accommodation lists.

Rights of Way: a guide to law and practice (John Trevelyan and John Riddall; Ramblers' Association 071-582 6878 / Open Spaces Society 0491-573535). Known as "The Blue Book". Contains 528 pages of summaries of legislation of relevance to walkers, enacted from 1982 to 1992.

Rights of Way: a guide to the law in Scotland (Scottish Rights of Way Society 031-652 2937). Clearly sets out the position of rights of way in Scotland, and the differences between the law in Scotland and that applying in England and Wales.

Walker's Handbook (Hugh Westacott; Oxford Illustrated Press 0865-790402). General information on all aspects of walking, including a good section on navigation. Useful reference sections on organisations and walking areas.

NAVIGATION

Follow the Map – An Ordnance Survey Guide (John G. Wilson; Ordnance Survey 0703-775555 / A.C. Black 0480-212666). A fascinating and beautiful book with many full colour map extracts and photographs. Gives an excellent feel for the principal navigational techniques, but lacks really practical advice.

Land Navigation: Routefinding with Map & Compass (Wally Keay; Duke of Edinburgh's Award Scheme 031-557 6657). One of the best books on map and compass for everyday walking. Aimed particularly at a young readership, but soundly covers the techniques needed for walking in "normal" and "wild" conditions.

Mountain Navigation (Peter Cliff; Cordee 0533-543579). The essentials of mountain navigation in the higher parts of Britain are well covered, with particularly good sections on estimating time and distance.

Mountain Navigation Techniques (Kevin Walker; Constable & Co 081-741 3663). A comprehensive and reliable guide to open country navigation and planning, packed with tips and much useful information.

Practical Moorland Navigation* (Don Bain; Bivvibug 0208-84649). An inexpensive resume in note form of all the basic techniques needed for open country navigation; full of practical and helpful advice.

Maps & Navigation* Ramblers' Association Factsheet 2 (Ramblers' Association 071-582 6878). Free. An introduction to Ordnance Survey maps, with basic map reading and route-finding techniques.

Simply Map Reading (Richard Neve; Ordnance Survey 0703-775555 / Telegraph Maps 071-538 5000). Sound technique for navigation. Full colour map extracts and diagrams. Some essential techniques omitted, such as setting the map. Rather brief compass section.

LEADERSHIP

Mountaincraft & Leadership (Eric Langmuir; Scottish Sports Council 031-317 7200 / Mountain Leader Training Board 061-273 5835). Covers navigation, hillwalking, security on steep ground, weather forecasting. Very good chapter on leadership.

ORGANISING & RUNNING A COURSE

Manual of Map Reading (Her Majesty's Stationery Office 071-873 0011). Aimed at instructors in the armed forces, but includes useful advice and information, especially on compass work and map setting. Also suggestions for indoor and outdoor exercises.

SUGGESTIONS FOR WALKING ROUTES

Long Distance Walker's Handbook (A.& C. Black 0480-212666). Summary of over 300 long distance routes throughout Britain, including details of guidebooks available.

No Through Road: The AA Book of Country Walks (Drive Publications 071-409 5225). Large, expensive loose-leaf compendium covering the whole of Britain. Individual walks can be taken out and carried in the plastic cover provided. Also includes a separate book containing general information on walking, and a pocket guidebook to flora and fauna.

Walker's Britain – Books 1 and 2 (Pan Books 071-373 6070 / Ordnance Survey 0703-775555). 240 routes in most parts of Britain. Also includes advice on general walking matters.

The following monthly magazines include route suggestions in various parts of Britain:

Country Walking (EMAP Pursuit Publishing 0858-468888)

The Great Outdoors (George Outram & Co. 0355-246444)

Outdoor (Mark Allen Publishing 081-671 7521)

APPENDIX 2 : AWARD SCHEMES AND COURSES

After following Sections A and B of this manual, you should have learned the basic requirements of navigation and leadership. If you wish to gain more knowledge and experience, with recognition of your progress in the form of an award or certificate, you should consider joining one of the following award schemes and courses.

Also, if you wish to navigate or lead in wild conditions (see Introduction, paragraph 10), you are strongly advised to undertake a suitable course.

We give a brief description of the relevant awards and courses that we know, together with contact details for further information. Inclusion in the list does not indicate a recommendation by the Ramblers' Association, and you are advised to obtain the organisers' literature to satisfy yourself that a scheme or course is suitable for your requirements.

AWARD SCHEMES

These are administered by a supervisory body, whose address is shown. They will supply further information and the course venues.

Basic Expedition Training Award. Central Council of Physical Recreation, Francis House, Francis Street, London, SW1P 1DE. 071-828 3163. This award is for youth workers and others who wish to train people in the basic skills involved in journeying on foot in the British Isles in the summer months. It also covers leading, and having responsibility for, parties – especially groups of young people – travelling in *non-wild* countryside. Courses cover leadership, party management, navigation, equipment, first aid and emergencies, weather, preparation, conservation, access, etc. The award is not designed as a mountain qualification.

Mountainwalking Leader Training Scheme (Summer). Mountain Leader Training Board, Crawford House, Precinct Centre, Booth Street East, Manchester, M13 9RZ. 061-273 5835. General advice and information is also available from the MLTB's Snowdonia office on 06904-272. This scheme, which can lead to a summer mountain leader award, is widely recognised and is valid throughout the UK. It promotes the safe enjoyment of the hills and provides training and assessment in the technical and group management skills required by those who wish to lead groups in the mountains and moorlands of the UK other than in winter conditions. A booklet containing the definitive list of Mountainwalking Leader courses approved by the MLTB can be obtained from the Board's office in Manchester. The principal centre for such courses is the Sports Council's mountain centre at Plas y Brenin, Capel Curig, Gwynedd, LL24 0ET. 06904-214.

Winter Mountain Leader Award. Scottish Mountain Leader Training Board, Caledonia House, South Gyle, Edinburgh, EH12 9DQ. 031-317 7200. This award covers the leadership of hillwalking parties under winter conditions.

European Mountain Leader Award. This award covers the provision of leading services for hillwalking parties within the European Community. ML Summer award holders are eligible to register for the award. It is administered by the UK Mountain Training Board, Capel Curig, Gwynedd, LL24 0ET. 06904-272

Further details of the above mountain leader awards, and of mountain instructor and ski leader awards, are contained in the UKMTB's **National Guidelines for Safety and Good Practice in Mountain and Related Activites.** This is a consultative document which should be studied in particular by those concernend with mountain safety and with the provision of instruction in mountain leadership.

National Navigation Award Scheme. British Orienteering Federation, Riversdale, Dale Road North, Darley Dale, Matlock, Derbyshire, DE4 2HX. 0629-734042. The scheme is available to people of all ages and abilities from children to veteran adults – to anyone in fact who seeks to explore the countryside with confidence and competence. It is arranged in three sections (bronze, silver and gold), each representing an achievement level validated to a national standard.

The Duke of Edinburgh's Award. Gulliver House, Madeira Walk, Windsor, SL4 1EU. 0753-810753. The Award is open to people between the ages of 14 and 23, providing a wide range of opportunities to challenge and develop the individual. It is run by volunteers for volunteers, so if you would enjoy sharing your navigating and walking skills with others, please make contact. The Expeditions Section of the Award is not designed as a qualification for leadership.

COURSES

Many Ramblers' Association areas and groups organise courses for members on map reading and/or leadership. They are usually publicised in the appropriate newsletters.

Courses are also offered to the general public by private companies and other organisations with qualified instructors. They are residential (unless shown otherwise) with accommodation included in the price, either at the organisation's own base, or at nearby hotels, guest houses etc. In most cases,these courses do not lead to recognised awards. Lists of courses which do lead to awards can be obtained from the award-supervising organisations referred to above.

The Ackers, Golden Hillock Road, Small Heath, Birmingham, B11 2PY. 021-771 4448. A variety of outdoor education courses including walking and navigational skills.

Bivvybug, Boscarhyn, Syra Close, St. Kew Highway, Bodmin, Cornwall, PL30 3ED. 0208-84649. Courses on moorland navigation and leadership for individuals and organised groups.

Country Venture Activities, The Old School, Tebay, Cumbria, CA10 3TP. 0587-4286. Weekend and three or four day courses for individuals and groups. Covers navigation for beginners and advanced.

Glenmore Lodge, Aviemore, Inverness-shire, PH22 1QU. 0479-861276. The Scottish Sports Council's outdoor training centre. Offers a wide variety of courses, including navigation and mountain leadership training.

High Trek Snowdonia, Tal-y-Waen, Deiniolen, Gwynedd, LL55 3NA. 0286-871232. Long weekends, mostly out on the hills, covering all aspects of navigation.

Highlander Mountaineering, Highlea, Auchnarrow, Glenlivet, Banffshire, AB37 9JN. 0807-590250. Combined one-week hillwalking and navigation courses for individuals in summer, based at Tomintoul at the foot of the Cairngorm Mountains. Includes a night out at a bothy or camping.

Kevin Walker Mountain Activity, 74 Beacons Park, Brecon, Powys, LD3 9BQ. 0874-625111. One or two day mountain navigation courses for beginners and advanced; also hillwalking leadership courses.

Ordnance Survey, Romsey Road, Maybush, Southampton, SO9 4DH. 0703-792331. Non-residential map skills courses for teachers in either one full-day or two half-day modules.

The Outward Bound Trust, Chestnut Field, Regent Place, Rugby, Warwickshire, CV21 2PJ. 0788-560423. Courses for all age groups at four centres in the Lake District, Scottish Highlands and mid Wales. The courses are multi-activity, and include mountain navigation as well as rock climbing, water-based activities and others.

Peak National Park Centre, Losehill Hall, Castleton, Derbyshire, S30 2WB. 0433-620373. Map and compass courses for beginners and intermediates, with theory in the classroom and practice on the moors. Also weekend rambling leadership courses, recommended by the RA.

Plas y Brenin (National Mountain Centre), Capel Curig, Gwynedd, LL24 0ET. 06904-214. Weekend map and compass courses for experienced walkers, and mountain leadership training courses.

Professional Mountaineering Services, Calluna, Heathercroft, Fort William, Inverness-shire, PH33 6RE. 0397-700451. Two-day courses in navigation and winter walking skills in the Scottish Highlands.

R & L Adventures, Knotts Farm, Patterdale Road, Windermere, Cumbria, LA23 1NL. 0539-445104. Tuition for individuals and groups; duration flexible. Orienteering, rockclimbing, abseiling, canoeing and potholing courses and mountain leadership training.

Ramblers Scotland Winter Training Programme, Crusader House, Markinch, Fife, KY7 6AQ. 0592-611177. A series of weekend courses held at the Kingussie bases of Scottish Mountain Guides and Sonnhalde / Avalanche Awareness (see below). The main skills taught are: basic training in the use of ice axe and crampons; navigation and mountain safety; appreciation of snow and ice conditions.

Scottish Mountain Guides, Airleywight, The Crescent, Kingussie, Inverness-shire, PH21 1JZ. 0540-661532. An independent guiding service which runs the Ramblers' Association's winter skills training courses in Scotland.

Sonnhalde / Avalanche Awareness, East Terrace, Kingussie, Inverness-shire, PH21 1JS. 0540-661266. A base for Ramblers' Association winter skills training courses as well as a wide variety of outdoor activity holidays.

South Shropshire Walking Holidays, Hill Cottage, The Bog, Stiperstones, Shropshire, SY5 0NL. 0743-791918. Walking holidays at various grades; also training in navigation and leadership skills by Brian Nelson. Small groups of about 6 people. Weekends a speciality.

Youth Hostels Association, 8 St.Stephen's Hill, St.Albans, Hertfordshire, AL1 2DY. 0727-845047/855215)

Scottish Youth Hostels Association, 7 Glebe Crescent, Stirling, FK8 2JA. 0786-451181.

Beginners and improvers weekend courses in map reading and orienteering based on a number of youth hostels.

PRIVATE TUTORS & CONSULTANTS

The following members of the Ramblers' Association's Panel of Advisers on Navigation and Leadership provide courses in map reading, but without certificate or award:

Chris Sweetman, 45g Nidderdale, Wollaton, Nottingham, NG8 2TN. 0602-287321. Holds Mountainwalking Leader and British Orienteering Federation certificates. Offers courses in navigation and leadership.

Julian Tippett, 40 Spencer Road, Isleworth, Middlesex, TW7 4BH. 081-560 4541. Runs map and compass courses at beginners and advanced levels in south west London, in Surrey and in West Sussex.

APPENDIX 3 : EQUIPMENT CHECK-LIST

As well as suitable footwear, waterproofs, rucksack and a spare sweater in case it turns cold, the leader and backmarker should also carry the following items. Most are quite small and light, and need not take up much room in your rucksack. Some may be needed rarely, but could save much trouble, or even a life, in an emergency.

ESSENTIAL ITEMS

Coins for essential telephone calls (also if possible a phonecard, though few country call boxes accept these).
Compass (paragraph 1.32).
First aid kit (paragraph 4.50).
Lightweight **foil blanket** or **bivouac** (bivvy) **bag** (paragraph 4.53vi).
Map (paragraphs 1.5 to 1.11).
Map protection (paragraph 1.14).
Notebook, pen and pencil for use during your reconnaissance and for anything that needs to be recorded on the day of the walk (paragraphs 2.50 to 2.54).
Ramblers' Association literature. Several copies of **the RA recruitment leaflet** and your area or group programme, for non-members in your party (paragraph 5.16).
Route card (paragraph 2.56).
Secateurs or **walking stick** (paragraph 4.21).
Spare clothing for yourself – and be prepared to lend it to others in an emergency.
Spare food, in case you are caught in bad weather, or for an emergency (paragraphs 4.35ii and 4.53vi).
Torch with spare battery and bulb, if the walk is likely to end at or near dusk (paragraphs 4.30 to 4.32). Also reflective armbands if possible.
Watch – to check that you are on schedule (paragraph 3.22).
Waterbottle
Whistle – to attract attention in emergency (paragraph 4.55).

OPTIONAL ITEMS

Binoculars for identifying distant stiles (paragraph 1.47) and items of interest.
"Dictaphone" for taking notes easily, especially on the reconnaissance.
Magnifying lens if you have difficulty reading small print (some compasses incorporate one).
Pocket knife The knife itself and sundry other attachments in the Swiss Army and similar types could be useful in a wide variety of situations.
Romer (paragraph 1.31) The baseplate of your compass may have one of these.

APPENDIX 4 : OBTAINING MAPS

You should be able to buy or order the full range of Ordnance Survey Landranger, Pathfinder and Outdoor Leisure series through any good bookseller. In case of difficulty, the Ordnance Survey (0703-792763/4) can provide details of their official agents in most cities and large towns.

The following are map specialists – all do mail order:

Cordee 3a De Montfort Street, Leicester, LE1 7HD. 0533-543579.

Edward Stanford 12 Long Acre, Covent Garden, London, WC2E 9LP. 071-836 1321.

HMSO Bookshops 49 High Holborn, London, WC1V 6HB. 071-873 0011
258 Broad Street, Birmingham, B1 2HE. 021-643 3179
33 Wine Street, Bristol, BS1 2BQ. 0272-264306
9 Princess Street, Manchester, M60 8AS. 061-834 7201
16 Arthur Street, Belfast, BT1 4GD. 2032-238451
71 Lothian Street, Edinburgh, EH3 9AZ. 031-228 4181

The Map Shop 15 High Street, Upton-on-Severn, WR8 0HJ. 0684- 593146.

Maps by Mail PO Box 291A, Surbiton, Surrey, KT5 9LX. 081-399 4970.

National Map Centre 22 Caxton Street, Westminster, London, SW1H 0QU. 071-222 2466.

Trident Map Services 70 High Street, Houghton Regis, Dunstable, LU5 5BJ. 0582-867211

The **Map Library of the Ramblers' Association** at its London office (see below) stocks the Landranger 1:50,000 and Outdoor Leisure 1:25,000 series, but not the Pathfinder 1:25,000 series. Sheets are available on loan to RA members only at a charge of 25p per map plus postage and packing, for a period of six weeks from the date of issue. Borrowers are responsible for returning maps in good condition, and will be charged for loss or damage.

To order maps, contact the Map Library Service*, at least ten days in advance if possible, stating the sheet number(s) of the maps required and your membership number. Please do not send any money with your order, as an invoice will be sent with the maps, to be paid when the maps are returned.

* Map Library Service, Ramblers' Association,
1/5 Wandsworth Road, London, SW8 2XX.
Phone 071-582 6878. Fax 071-587 3799.

Public libraries usually have Landranger and Outdoor Leisure maps for loan. These are sometimes laminated thereby providing extra protection in wet weather.

APPENDIX 5 : MORE USEFUL ADDRESSES

Ramblers' Association
1/5 Wandsworth Road, London, SW8 2XX.
Phone 071-582 6878. Fax 071-587 3799

Ramblers' Association (Wales)
Pantwood, Pant Lane, Marford, Wrexham, Clwyd, LL12 8SG. Phone 0978-855148. Fax 0978-852764

Ramblers' Association (Scotland)
Crusader House, Haig Business Park, Markinch, Fife, KY7 6AQ. Phone 0592-611177. Fax 0592-611188

For addresses of RA Area and Group Contacts, please refer to the section under this heading in the Rambler's Yearbook and Accommodation Guide (free to all members, and available on sale at bookshops).

Countryside Commission
John Dower House, Crescent Place, Cheltenham, Gloucestershire, GL50 3RA.
Phone 0242-521381*. Fax 0242-584270
(* For publications call 0604-781848)

Countryside Council for Wales/
Cymgor Cefn Gwlad Cymru
Plas Penrhos, Ffordd Penrhos, Bangor, Gwynedd, LL57 2LQ.
Phone 0248-370444. Fax 0248-355782

Scottish Natural Heritage
12 Hope Terrace, Edinburgh, EH9 2AS.
Phone 031-447 4784. Fax 031-446 2279

British Mountaineering Council
Crawford House, Precinct Centre, Booth Street East, Manchester, M13 9RZ. Phone 061-273 5835

Mountaineering Council for Scotland
71 King Street, Crieff, PH7 3HB. Phone 0764 4962

NATIONAL TOURIST BOARDS IN THE UNITED KINGDOM

England Thames Tower, Black's Road, London, W6 9EL. Phone 081-846 9000. Fax 081-563 0302

Northern Ireland St.Anne's Court, 59 North Street, Belfast, BT1 1NB. Phone 0232-231221. Fax 0232-240960

Scotland 23 Ravelston Terrace, Edinburgh, EH4 3EU. Phone 031-332 2433. Fax 031-343 1513

Wales (Bwrdd Croeso Cymru) Brunel House, 2 Fitzalan Road, Cardiff CF2 1UY. Phone 0222-499909

Guernsey (including Alderney, Herm and Sark). PO Box 23, White Rock, Guernsey, Channel Islands Phone 0481-726611. Fax 0481-721246

Jersey Liberation Square, St.Helier, Jersey, Channel Islands Phone 0534-500700. Fax 0534-500808

Isle of Man Sea Terminal Building, Douglas, Isle of Man Phone 0624-686801. Fax 0624-686800

REGIONAL TOURIST BOARDS IN THE UNITED KINGDOM

Cumbria Ashleigh, Holly Road, Windermere, Cumbria, LA23 2AQ.
Phone 0539-444444. Fax 0539-444041

East Anglia Toppesfield Hall, Hadleigh, Suffolk, IP7 5DN. Phone 0473-822922. Fax 0473-823063

East Midlands Exchequergate, Lincoln, LN2 1PZ. Phone 0522-531521. Fax 0522-532501

Heart of England Woodside, Larkhill Road, Worcester, WR5 2EF. Phone 0905-763436. Fax 0905-763450

London 26 Grosvenor Gardens, London, SW1W 0DU. Phone 071-730 3450. Fax 071-730 9367

North West Swan House, Swan Meadow Road, Wigan Pier, Wigan, WN3 5BB. Phone 0942-821222. Fax 0942-820002

Northumbria Aykley Heads, Durham, DH1 5UX. Phone 091-384 6905. Fax 091-386 0899

South East England Old Brew House, Warwick Park, Tunbridge Wells, Kent, TN2 5TU.
Phone 0892-540766. Fax 0892-511008

Southern 40 Chamberlayne Road, Eastleigh, Hampshire, SO5 5JH. Phone 0703-620006. Fax 0703-620010

West Country 60 St. David's Hill, Exeter, Devon, EX4 4SY.
Phone 0392-76351. Fax 0392-420891

Yorkshire & Humberside 312 Tadcaster Road, York, YO2 2HF. Phone 0904-707961. Fax 0904-701414

NATIONAL TOURIST OFFICES in London of European countries:

Belgium 29 Princes Street, London, W1R 7RG.
Phone 071-629 0230. Fax 071-629 0454

Denmark Sceptre House, 169 Regent Street, London, W1R 8PY. Phone 071-734 2637. Fax 071-494 2170

France 178 Piccadilly, London, W1V 0AL.
Phone 071-499 6911. Fax 071-493 6594

Germany Nightingale House, 65 Curzon Street, London, W1Y 7PE. Phone 071-495 3990. Fax 071-495 6129

Irish Republic 150 New Bond Street, London, W1Y 0AQ.
Phone 071-493 3201. Fax 071-493 9065

Netherlands P O Box 523, London, SW1E 6LD.
Phone 0891-200 277 (premium rate). Fax 071-828 7941

OTHER ORGANISATIONS

The addresses and telephone numbers of a large number of organisations concerned with outdoor recreation, conservation etc., are shown in the Address Directory of the Rambler's Yearbook and Accommodation Guide.

Index

References to paragraphs take this form (e.g.):

2.11 refers to module 2, paragraph 1

I 10 refers to Introduction, paragraph 10

PE 1.6 refers to Practical Exercise 6, module 1

Also: "M" = module; app. = appendix; fig. = figure.